MW01658182

Field Notes

and Other Stories...

-Mike Lunsford-

Shade Tree Press
8945 South Coxville Rd.
Rosedale, Indiana 47874
www.mikelunsford.com

©Copyright 2017 by Mike Lunsford
All rights reserved

Printed in the United States of America

The author and publisher gratefully acknowledge the ***Terre Haute Tribune-Star*** in which the contents of this book appeared in column form.

Library of Congress Control Number: 2017909781

Front cover art, *The Back 40*, courtesy of the artist, K. Nash DisPennett. Additional cover and title page art by Page Fetter. Author's photo by Joan Lunsford.

Lunsford, Michael J. (Mike), 1956-
Field Notes and Other Stories... / Mike Lunsford
ISBN (pbk.) 978-0-692-91115-0

To our new grandson, Joseph;
may we be friends forever.

-Foreward-

The first story in this book is "On the Art of Field Notes," and I arrived at writing it because I realized one day last spring that I was no longer taking a notebook with me on my daily walks. I'm not sure when I got out of the habit, but it has become a bad one, not quite like an addiction, but sloppy and lazy nonetheless.

I usually have a camera with me now as I venture onto the road or out into the woods, but there are some instances when a picture really isn't worth a thousand words, and I should quit abusing my chosen craft of working with words for the sake of a new passion. Of course, reading what I jot down in a notebook is a whole other story, for it is nearly always illegible.

It is an interesting note to add here that a handwriting analyst friend of mine says that although my scrawl hasn't changed much in the past five years—when she first took a look at it for a story I wrote—she does now see a "suggestion" in my penmanship of "wanting space" in my life. She says that trend is shown by the larger gaps I am leaving between my lines. I suppose her comments are just one more reason I have seriously considered giving up my day job as a teacher before long, for I am wanting more independence to do what I want to do with fewer strings attached.

We realize that the woods we own—about 15 acres of them—are really just ours for a while; we will eventually get too old to take care of our place and hand it off to someone else. We are considering some sort of an agreement to which the new owners must consent to never log the trees we have watched grow for most of the last 40 years. Like everyone else, I could use some ready cash, but it would haunt me if I ever saw our timber cut; I'd be robbing my grandchildren of something special, I think.

A lifetime ago I roamed a completely different kind of topography near my childhood home. While here there is clay and rock and gravel, and steep hillsides that lead down to mushy and cattail-choked wetlands, there and then it was sandy meadows and orchards and old growth oaks and tulip poplars. Although I love my land—particularly its birds and turtles, and its long-abandoned railroad grade and cottonwoods, I treasure the memory of the woods I grew up with. The sunlight seemed to filter through the trees differently there, and I believe that all these years later I could still walk straight to its best spots, although a while ago a logger "harvested" what was best about those special places, and I know it can never be the same.

It may be some form of old-age regression, but I believe I may have spent more time in the woods in the past six months than at any other time since I was very young and wore patched jeans and fancied myself some sort of Daniel Boone. Although I never "kilt a bar" and left my carvings in a beech tree to mark the spot, I knew our woods like the back of my hand, whether that be a cliché or not. I read a passage from the scientist Jane Goodall in which she referred to a favorite tree, "Beech," as a friend. That may sound a bit crazy to some, but not to me.

So, as I step toward retirement, and as I venture down into my woods, I have had field notes in mind, and not just those I scribble into a reporter's notebook either. I mean the reflective sort, the contemplative kind that involves not only what I see on any given day of walking, but what I saw years ago and far away, only in time, not distance; the collective sort that is tucked away in the folds of memory.

This book is yet another collection of the stories I tell. They come from experiences and encounters, both new and old. Quite simply, it has two parts: the first comprised of stories written with nature and being out-of-doors in mind, and the second, a collection of everything else my editor found worthy of making the cut.

Well, then off we go on another adventure, and I can't do that without thanking everyone involved in this book: the artists who contributed to its cover, the friends who endorsed it, my wife, Joanie, who inspired it, and, of course, my readers, who I hope find it worthy of their bookshelves... **ML**

-Table of Contents-

Chapter 1 – Field Notes

Chapter 2 – Other Stories

"...stories swim by the millions, and most of being a writer is listening and seeing, and then madly scribbling."

Brian Doyle

Field Notes

and Other Stories...

Shade Tree Press

CHAPTER ONE: FIELD NOTES

On the Art of Field Notes

May 22, 2017

I don't know if in the years to come I will have to rely on taking more notes as I walk and talk my way toward stories. I am hopeful of holding on to enough of my functioning brain cells for a good while yet, but just in case, perhaps I should begin carrying a notebook with me, as I used to when I was new to this business. Even before that, I carried one in an uncle's old Army-issue knapsack and roamed imaginary jungles; I wish I had those notebooks now.

My scrawled notes have little in common with the great field journals of the immortal naturalists. I've seen pages from Charles Darwin's notebooks, and those of Meriweather Lewis and Henry David Thoreau, and ever hoping to draw a bird or fish or turtle, as they did—or even write as legibly—is a pipe dream. I can draw a decent leaf, a passable tree, a reasonable cloud, but anything with four legs or gills or whiskers could very well resemble a Rorschach inkblot if I sketch it.

Pencil and paper are losing their influences in

our learning lives, so much that this old devoted book reader has to sadly admit that he often can't decipher his own handwriting. So I decided a long time ago to most often forgo a note pad and pen for memory only, although I usually have one handy for interviews.

I love our language, treasure its power and rue its passing impact on a digitalized populace; yet I must, within a day or so of taking notes, transcribe my scribbles onto a nicely formatted computer document, usually in Times New Roman font, of course.

That all considered, I realized last weekend as I walked along the grassy and tie-less railroad grade below our house, that I had nothing to write on or with, and it seemed at that very moment that everywhere I looked I saw something significant, things that were story-worthy and interesting.

The morning was cool, and a breeze blowing out of the north brought the wonderful scent of rosa multiflora from the scrub that skirts my shallow pond; its white and yellow flowers were already hosting an abundance of bees and flies. I recalled just then that not long ago an old-timer (that's anyone older than I am) told me that locomotives used to take on water at that spot, and I pictured that in my head, knowing that the place where I stood hardly looks as it did when the old steam engines of the Chicago and Eastern Illinois chugged along to Roseville and points north.

I still find the carcasses of rotted ties and an occasional spike or cinder along the way, and I know that there are huge trees along the path—mostly sycamores and cottonwoods—that were just head high when squealing whistles and firemen's shouts were heard there.

I was in no hurry as I stared into the now-leaved trees for birds; I glanced down at my boots too, for a week before a snake had slithered across my feet there. Within five minutes I was rewarded when I spied a green heron sitting in an oak tree; he was intensely staring across the water at something, and I was soon so engrossed in watching him watch something else that I hardly realized—until it was too late—that a Great Blue Heron was no more than 30 feet behind me, preening and fishing before the sun got too high in the sky. As I turned I caught his squawking exit and missed my chance for a picture; the old grouch flew over a stand of trees that blocked my view.

My attention was soon back to the roosted bird, when a hummingbird, its blue-green chest feathers shining in the sun, lit on a naked branch. Her appearance reminded me to remind Joanie that the time had come to get sugar water on the stove and prepare our feeders for summer guests.

I also made mental notes of beech and live oak saplings, of cedars the height of a yardstick and a cottonwood too tall to even guess its height. Along the way I noted the greening of the poison ivy, the ferns that had doubled in size in a week or so, the horsetails — both male and female — that always remind me of the neatly drawn prehistoric swamps, complete with razor-toothed dinosaurs, that inhabited the pages of a

"Golden Nature Guide" I used to carry in that aforementioned knapsack. I still have that book on a cabin shelf.

There was a pleasantness about those morning woods that allowed me to push my waiting work aside. It is one thing to be among the trees and brush and mucky water of a wetlands when it is barely 70 degrees, but a whole other idea—and feel—when it has reached 90 and the air is heavy with water. My thoughts turned to what the itch and humidity of that very place would feel like in July or August.

I spent nearly three hours walking and gawking and listening, and of that time, I can't seem to recall what occupied my mind; it certainly wasn't work. I have been keeping my eyes on a pair of young red-tailed hawks for weeks, so I visited with them a bit, and I walked in both directions to listen to the gurgles of a pair of rusty-red coal mine springs, their iron-tinted water seeming to have no effect on the hearty life of the toothwort and trillium that grows nearby.

After I had made it back to my doorstep, I decided that despite remembering a few things, I suppose it wouldn't hurt if I started to tuck a notebook in the camera backpack I carry into the woods. I may not be able to read but every third word I record, and I probably won't waste my time in drawing much, unless someone with infinite patience is willing to teach me.

I can live with never being an Audubon or Muir or Burroughs—they were all tougher than I am anyway—but I can identify a little with E.O. Wilson, the old ant-hunting naturalist who recently wrote the forward to a book about notebooks called *Field Notes on Science and Nature*.

He says: "If there is a heaven, and I am allowed entrance, I will ask for no more than an endless living world to walk through and explore. I will carry with me an inexhaustible supply of notebooks, from which I can send back reports to the sedentary spirits."

There's a Good Reason to Grow Weeds

July 5, 2015

Years and years ago, not long after I had begun my working life without a hay wagon involved, I took a job at a new restaurant in town that sat next to a weed-choked lot. The manager of the place wanted volunteers to go clean up the mess, and I, who thoroughly liked being outdoors, but already equally disliked slapping burgers on buns, had my hand in the air first.

It was a hot and itchy job, but at least I could work at my own pace and to the sounds of birds and bugs, so I started hacking and chopping and mowing as if leading Sir Richard Burton toward Lake Tanganyika. But on the second day of the job, I had quite a surprise. Sweating in the sun amid a stand of giant ragweed, I looked up to see my manager studying the weeds as if assaying timber.

"Why are ya' cutting these trees down?" he asked me. "They're not trees; they're weeds," I replied, knowing he was from out of state.

"Nice-lookin' weeds," he said. "Do you think a few of those would live in my yard?"

Now, I wasn't going to argue with the man; after all, he was paying me nearly two bucks an hour (enough in those days to buy a movie ticket or a quarter of a tank of gas), so I dutifully pulled a few of the heartiest specimens up by the roots, wrapped them in wet newspaper, and tossed them in the trunk of his car. I never asked him how his venture in weed cultivation panned out.

All these years later, I am still a puller of weeds. I try to not use sprays around my place, but I could win a county fair blue ribbon with my ability to yank weeds; it is a skill honed by a neatnik mother who liked her flower beds clean. Now I often cut my weeds with a gas-powered, industrial-sized trimmer, and take great satisfaction in clearing a nice, neat border between where my woods end and my yard begins. That is, until I started planting weeds instead.

I am cultivating milkweed these days—in fact, two kinds of it. You see, common milkweed (Asclepias syriaca) and whorled milkweed (Asclepias verticillata), two of the six or seven types of the stuff, serve as both food and housing for monarch butterflies, and those, unlike my former boss's weed of choice, I want in my yard. In fact, if we want to keep seeing monarchs around, we all need to set aside a patch of dirt alongside our yards or gardens and encourage milkweed to grow there. Monarchs are in trouble, and one of the main reasons why is because milkweed is disappearing too.

Of course, one reason the plant is troubled is because it is labeled as a "weed," the definition for which, according to the Merriam-Webster Dictionary, is "an obnoxious growth, thing, or person," and "a plant that is not valued where it is growing." For the most part then, milkweed is, indeed, a weed, so it is sprayed and mowed, and, in the case of land development, completely eradicated by concrete and asphalt, bricks and mortar.

"A weed is any plant that is out of place. Corn growing in a soybean field is a weed," says Phil Cox, Vermillion County's Extension Agriculture and Natural Resources Educator, who also happens to be an expert in prairie plants and wildlife, and my brother-in-law, although he may not claim the latter title. He's willing to speak to anyone who will listen about native plants and wildlife, and it was from Phil and the Wabash Valley Audubon Society that I purchased my whorled milkweed seedlings.

"It's amazing that if you plant one or 10 or 20 milkweed plants, monarchs will somehow find and lay eggs on them, and their larvae will hatch. So we need to plant more native milkweed to help them survive," Cox told me while he watched it rain at a soggy Boy Scout camp near Sheridan last week.

Why monarchs are attracted to such a relatively unattractive plant as milkweed isn't completely known, but a favored chapter in Allen Young's *Small Creatures and Ordinary Places* (University of Wisconsin Press, 2000), a book from which I have quoted with near biblical reverence in the past, comes as close to anything I have ever read.

"The monarch butterfly is found across the entire continent, due in large part to the fact that its caterpillar food, a diverse group of herbaceous plants called milkweeds, is also widely distributed… The caterpillar chews the succulent, white latex sap-filled milkweed leaves and grows in a matter of weeks. Then it shrinks a bit, spins a button of silk on a twig or stem, (often not on milkweed), snares a rear clasper in it, hangs down, and splits its skin, exposing a beautiful green chrysalis."

Young explains everything you'd ever want to know about monarchs and milkweed, including the fact that the butterfly apparently thrives on the plant's "cardiac glycosides," a chemical that is repellant to most monarch predators.

He explains that there are essentially three generations of monarchs that develop from early spring when they leave Mexico for the southern states, to when they leave their northernmost climes to head south of the border again. He says they are the symbol of a season that is itself an "ecological minefield," and that the butterflies are in trouble—like so many other plants and animals—because humans are destroying their habitats.

Seeing that he had no place to go that didn't involve getting damp, Cox also added, "It would be great if people, besides planting milkweed, would also plant golden rod and asters; they help with the fall migration of monarchs as nectar sources. Many people buy chrysanthemums in the fall, but they really aren't good pollinators; buy the asters instead. I go to nurseries in the fall, and mums create little bio deserts. Look at where the bees and flies and butterflies are. It's not around the mums. We should be planting classic prairie flowers, like prairie blazing star and rough blazing star too." And, milkweed.

I have come to believe that my management of nature most encourages beauty, and I'll not stop mowing and trimming and picking and cleaning anytime soon. But I do intend to continue to cultivate my weed patch too, for it is there, in the summer heat, amid the drooping heads of golden rod and faded and torn milkweed that beauty comes to visit us.

Mowing Grass During the Monsoon Season
July 20, 2015

It is nearly the midway point in this Indiana summer of ours, or as we have come to call it up my way: monsoon season in Bangladesh.

It rained again last night, and just a few hours ago, a storm blew through north of my place and left us with another half an inch. The weatherman says there's a good chance for more rain in the next few days, but I was pleasantly surprised to see bright yellow suns on his forecast for the week ahead.

I can recall only a few summers when we have

had this much rain, and one came in mid-August nearly 20 years ago. We had to miss a few days of school when our back-country gravel roads could take no more water.

I remember one particular morning when I headed off to work and had to turn around a mile or so from the house, for I could go in no other direction, except backward.

Of course, along with the rain this summer has come all of the extra amenities: mosquitoes the size of bats, gnat swarms that can double as low-hanging clouds, and three-shirts-a-day humidity levels.

And, grass; all of it I can handle. So much grass that my mowers and trimmers have taken on a haggard and grungy look, for when I am done with each new round of clipping and snipping, I neglect cleaning them up in lieu of standing under a shower nozzle.

By the time I have shed soaked jeans and shirt in our garage, I am already thinking about when I will be able to mow the yard again, particularly if I have had the temerity to watch the latest weather updates.

Just a few days ago, as I plumped my mower's tires with a little air and checked its oil, I noticed a small drip from one of its hydraulic pumps. I felt betrayed rather than annoyed, for the machine has been treated well and maintained according to its owner's manual. It, in turn, has never failed to do its job, not once; it is a zero-turn model with a mowing deck made from battleship steel, I believe.

But rather than push my luck by tinkering with

it myself, I called a repair shop, thinking that I had no business messing with something that complicated. It seems as if just about everyone else's mowers are showing similar stresses, for the mechanic, his garage filled to the ceiling with other hard-luck cases, suggested I might get mine back in time to mow next spring, that is if my repair loan is approved.

Determined to "do no harm," I decided to try to remedy the problem myself, and, surprisingly, now have it back and mowing, drip-free. I actually believe the mower resented my sudden handiness; it was looking for a few weeks of rest.

Comparing a little yard mowing to the tragedy of a home swept away by floodwaters, or the costs of swamped cornfields—over which many of my farmer friends are losing sleep—or the tension of fretting over a leaking roof or wet basement (tarpaulin and sump pump sales must surely be soaring), smacks of whining, so I'll try to simply complain instead.

I usually enjoy mowing, particularly in the spring and fall, when it is cooler. I realize that I risk being forced into a serious mental health evaluation when I say such an outrageous thing, but it's true. I get great satisfaction out of a nicely trimmed lawn. This summer, however, has proven to me that one can get too much of a good thing.

Our yard is a particularly difficult one to mow. First, it is about the size of Connecticut, and much of it must be trimmed by hand since it is mostly straight up and down and runs along our woods. I hacked the brush and briars back years ago, when I was a younger man, determined to have more of a back yard, and I am now paying for the view.

My backyard trimming usually takes the better part of an hour of literally bench pressing my push mower along our hillsides, the sweat and itch of July and August heat supplying me with quite an aerobic workout. I am thinking I should have a beach body by late August if this rain keeps up.

Several of my friends have mowing businesses, a money-making fever that I thankfully got over by the time I was 18 or so. One buddy tells me that he has mowed more grass this year than he ever has, and he regularly has had to mow it wet, even while it's pouring.

I have vowed that I will never mow wet grass, not unless it begins to rain while I am trying to finish the job; wet grass is hard on mower belts and blades and decks, and it leads to even more time with my head shoved under a mower deck as I scrape away a warm, moldy, ammonia-scented mess.

I often see folks—and realize they may be forced to do so by heavy work schedules—running a mower through grass so wet and so thick it looks like they're baling spinach dip instead of grass. I almost feel sorry for their poor mowers as they belch the stuff out of crud-choked chutes.

Living in Indiana, I imagine we'll be getting a different weather pattern moving in before long. We'll dry out and heat up, and before we know it, we'll wish we had a little of this rain to wash things off and cool us down and green our yards. By then we'll be complaining about the choking dust and nasty ground hornets and brutal sun.

It's tough work, but it still beats shoveling snow when we get to blizzard season.

Nothing Routine About July's Blue Moon

August 17, 2015

With predictable sameness, my wife and I leave our house in the evening through the summer months to walk our roads. We are told by our doctor with each yearly physical that our daily paces must be working well for us for our blood pressures and cholesterol counts and general fitness seem to satisfy him, despite his belief that I am just a bit too fond of cookies and cake.

To beat the heat, we have gotten into the routine of walking in the same hour that the sun sets, a habit that becomes necessary now, anyway, as we've headed back to our classrooms and the grading and after-school meetings associated with our jobs.

So, as has become our practice, we took to the asphalt in July a little before 9 o'clock, knowing we'd be heading home to the silent flicker of our night light, it serving the dual purpose of both illuminating our way and warning drivers that a pair of near-geriatric hoofers in yellow neon T-shirts is coming at them along the ditches.

It was uncharacteristically cool in the evenings that closed July. Despite daytime temperatures that ran near 90 degrees, and humidity that nearly matched those numbers, we found the evenings breezy and cool and comfortable, so that the miles that fled under our feet went easily, pleasantly.

For a solid week, the setting sun painted pictures worthy of an art museum, and it was a joy to be outside to see and hear and smell it. We have taken – for the sake of breaking out of a bit of a rut – to walking in any one of three directions, and on the 30th, we headed south toward town.

The first and last part of that route includes a stretch of road that has taken on the feel of a tunnel, for the fields that line both sides are green with corn, their stalks now 7 or 8 feet tall, perhaps even taller. Big, fat dragonflies swooped and darted between the tunnel's sides, slurping up what they could find, and they gave the place an almost pre-historic atmosphere, minus the swamp muck and horsetails.

As we clopped along, we caught sight of the moon as it rose over the top of the corn, growing, it seemed to us, bigger and bolder as we moved.

"Tomorrow night is the blue moon," Joanie announced to me, breaking the near silence that we both enjoyed. Even though I knew what the term meant, I was clueless that earlier in the month we had walked under a full moon then, too. I had simply forgotten, and besides, was lost in my own thoughts.

"I should bring a camera," I believe I said, then

promptly forgot that, too, more enamored with the glow of a pink-orange sunset and the book I wanted to finish that night.

The following evening, the moon took center stage, since we walked after a trip to town for supper. As we moved through the homestretch of the green tunnel, we craned our necks to see it as it peeked out above the purple-white corn tassels that take on the heavy, musky scent of summer. It was a clear night, and the breeze stirred the corn stalks like a milling crowd.

The phenomenon we call a blue moon rarely means that the moon, itself, is blue, although on some historic occasions that has been exactly the case. The eruption of Mount St. Helens in 1980 and Indonesia's Krakatoa, nearly a hundred years earlier, were two instances when ash clouds changed the way millions saw the moon through smoky, filtered light.

The modern interpretation of the blue moon is that it's "the second full moon in the same calendar month." The moon comes full every 29.5 days, which means that if there is a full moon early in a given month, another could fall in its very latest days. We had a full moon on July 2, as well. Of course, I hadn't remembered it, either, nor will I probably remember that similar circumstances will make it happen again in 2018.

The second, more archaic, definition is more complex: A blue moon occurs when it is the "third full moon in a season that has four." This extra moon — a

13th in a year's time—wreaks havoc on the ecclesiastical calendar, which gives names to the normal 12 moons. By simply referring to it as a "blue moon," the calendar could stay on track, and thus probably led to the term being applied to something that is relatively rare. By the way, blue moons can occur twice in a year—the last time coming in 1999.

By the time we'd had our baths and had begun to think of bed, the moon was above the treetops, and more than once we walked outside to look and appreciate and take photos of it. My mind wandered back to the times my big brother and I used our mail-order telescope to gaze toward the stars, focusing most often on a moon that, in those days, was still an absolute mystery; it was untouchable then, for man had not yet left his footprints or his flag on it.

Standing in the gravel of my driveway that night, I felt pretty much the same way. I was in awe of the moon and its "silver loneliness" all those years ago; I still am.

Improving on the Art of Seeing Things

September 28, 2015

A fresh breeze kicked up as I sat on a backyard hillside last Wednesday evening. It's not that I didn't have much to do. Rather, I had too much.

Nonetheless, I sat on for a while, listening to that bit of wind as it rattled the wild cherry and black walnut leaves, some of which, already as gold as fall wanted them to be, sifted about me like a light rain. At that moment, I could think of nowhere else I would have rather been.

It had been nearly hot just a few hours before, but the calendar and a light wind from the north gave birth to autumn that day. Although most of my trees remained summertime green, I realized then that I had already been seeing and feeling the fall, particularly when I've noticed the spider webs spun from nearly every downspout on the house, most hanging heavy with dew in the mornings.

We have seen full hummingbird feeders, too, normally an unusual sight, but now our friends are packing and leaving us day by day, their tables set but mostly unused.

The fencerows we walk past in the evenings are alive with sounds we don't usually hear until fall, mostly crickets and katydids, desperate for one last fling before proving their mortalities.

And our geraniums have taken on the prettiest blooms of the year, as if they, too, know that the frost, which always takes us by surprise, is surely on its way.

In the mornings, most often before the sun is up over the ridge of trees to the east and fully awake, I make my way north to work.

I often see a thick mist as it hangs over the Big Raccoon, the twisting creek that ambles, even more slowly than I do, along the soybean and corn fields. The steam rising off the warm brown water is a sure sign of fall, too, and sometimes, if I have left home a bit later than usual and the sun is already on the horizon, I stop along the road just to watch a little while.

I know that some of my neighbors, a few on their way to work, others up early for a cup of coffee and a little café conversation, may think as they drive past that I am a bit addled. But it is about as quiet and peaceful as my day gets, and I will have it, no matter what anyone else thinks.

In 1908, naturalist John Burroughs wrote "The Art of Seeing Things," the first in a series of essays on nature included in *Leaf and Tendril*, just one of his more than two dozen books. Past 70 by the time he wrote it, Burroughs had come to believe that in their haste to make both a life and a living, his countrymen were beginning to ignore the lessons and beauty of the natural world.

One modern editor, writing in reference to Burroughs' essay said, "Its quietness works quite powerfully in our over-amplified moment."

Burroughs believed that we all need to take the time to look at things closely, to watch and listen and observe. There is a wholesomeness in it and a peace that comes from it.

"Some people seem born with eyes in their heads, and others with buttons or painted marbles, and no amount of science can make one equal to the other in the art of seeing things," he wrote.

And so, I have taken to improving that "art," by taking the time to watch the morning mist on a muddy creek and sitting on a hillside amid a shower of golden leaves.

I am also beginning to haul my camera along on my walks, so that I may keep a little of what I have seen, particularly scenes of the most temperate seasons that always encourage me when the snows come blowing against my door and even an extra pair of socks can't keep my feet warm.

I have made a resolution, one that can't wait for the new year, and, perhaps, one I have already been practicing for a while, and that is to pay attention, to look at details, to improve at the commission of the art of seeing things.

It is not just writers like old John Burroughs who need to work at such things; we all do. We often lead such busy lives that we drive past treasures, overlook the beautiful, ignore the splendid. As I age, I suppose slowing down is inevitable, but for right now, at least at times, it has become intentional.

As Joanie and I made our way up a steep grade near dusk last Saturday night, an owl—a rare sight for us—slipped out of the dead branches of an elm tree that had been reserved all summer for a scarlet tanager, whose song we had enjoyed for the better part of a month. Joanie hadn't seen the owl, for by the time I told her to look toward the west to catch it in the fading sunlight, it had dipped into the darkness and was gone.

We walked on home, watching the sun set in a gorgeous red-orange glow, the same sunset we've witnessed countless times along the same horizon, framed by the same trees. Yet I felt this one was somehow different than any we'd ever seen, new and unique. I think I am learning well.

Enough Rain to Last a While
October 4, 2015

It is a gray and cold and miserable day as I sit in the warmth of my little writing space, occasionally looking over my right shoulder through a big window.

It is a most dreary scene: naked trees and flooded fields as far as I can see below us to the east. My place is perched on a hill, and if I am reading my topographic map correctly, it is on one of the highest spots in Parke County.

A promontory is a good place to be today, for what I am seeing looks more like Raccoon Lake than the creeping floodwaters of Big Raccoon Creek that pour over its banks like a big belly over a too-tight belt.

Mine is a county that has more than its share of gravel roads and covered bridges, shallow ditches and winding creeks—not to mention our fair stretch of the Wabash River—so the rain we have seen in recent days has become a preoccupation for us.

I realize that by the time this story runs in the paper, the flood (by most estimates well short of historic proportions) that we are contending with may very well be old news, that we may be dried out some by the sun that is supposed to show up in a few days.

But for today, anyway, the rain and rising currents here are the talk of everyone I meet, for a few folks I know have already found out what can happen when their sump pumps fail or their usual ways to work are hidden under brown water.

I noted in my last story that Joanie and I are going to purchase kayaks soon; had we done that earlier, we could have paddled our way through flooded fields to work this week, although thoughts of an accidental dunking leave me shivering. Paddling a calm lake or lazy stream is an altogether different thing than scooting a kayak through fast-moving floodwaters, so even if we had our new toys at hand, we'd be staying put and using our common sense.

We are used to seeing the Big Raccoon spilling out of itself, most often shutting off traffic through the old Roseville Bridge, then north again at another crook in the creek at Mecca. Not much farther north than that, a flooded Wabash River pushes the Big Raccoon backward, and I have seen the water near their confluence appearing addled and confused, not certain as to which way it wants to go.

That is one reason why, closer to home, we are watching our fields fill up, for the creek, like most of us when it comes to working hard, takes the course of least resistance.

For all of their inconvenience, these fairly frequent floods through my valley prove useful. The fields that now lay under shallow but frothy water produce plentiful corn and soybean crops when dried out come summer. That old creek deposits rich silt in the fields along its path, but it also does more than its fair share of twisting and turning, too.

The Big Raccoon seems to re-channel itself in

times like these, making it a stranger of sorts until we see it up close in the spring. For much of the summer, the work of the Army Corps of Engineers bottles the lake that feeds the creek, so we are introduced to sandbars and shallow places where before there were none.

Because of the scouring and boiling of these winter floods, there will be surprisingly deep spots in the creek where they didn't exist just a few months before, and floodwaters sweep the creek clear of debris as well. When the water drops after the spring rains, we look at the Big Raccoon's gravel and mussels and root-gnarled banks with new eyes.

Sugar Creek, with its sandstone bluffs and its nearness to Shades and Turkey Run state parks, may be a more beautiful stream than the Big Raccoon, but geologically, the latter can equal the former with a history that reaches back just as far.

One reason I can see so much water from my elevated spot is that I am within a healthy walk of where the Little Raccoon—which gets its start in Putnam County—and the Big Raccoon come together.

That spot is very much like a place where one road T's into another, and among the creek's most idiosyncratic of quirks, it is near there that this conjoined stream decides to cease a generally southwesterly direction and veer off to the northwest before it meets the Wabash miles later.

I am told that engineers and hydrologists have marveled at the creek's odd behavior. To the best of my knowledge, the Big Raccoon is navigable for over 40 miles, nearly all of them susceptible to flooding when we get rain as we have this week.

Much smaller streams nearby take on multiple personalities in these flooded days, too. Not two or three weeks ago, I parked my truck along Snow Road and scrambled down the side of what we call "the Twin Bridges."

I walked up a branch of shallow Spring Creek that runs under the bridges, camera in hand, hardly getting my boots muddy in the process. Nowhere did I see water more than six inches deep, yet today it is a raging torrent. I have seen water running within inches of the bottoms of those bridges, that laconic little stream a dangerous place for a few days.

Although there are undoubtedly some local cases, I know of no one here who has had to put up with anything more than a wet basement or leaking roof or inconvenient route to work. That is not the case for many poor people through Illinois and Missouri who, as I write this, are dealing with floods of epic proportions. Tornadoes and blizzards and thunderstorms have, these past few days, produced a three-headed monster of misery for folks not that far from us, and I'm sure a little more rain may soon prove to be a tipping point for those along the Wabash.

It was nearly dark when I stepped out of the warmth onto my deck to see that it had stopped raining. Not far below me in the woods, I heard the trilling of a Carolina wren, happy, I guess, for the sudden change in the weather. We may be high and dry where we are right now, but I think I can say without argument that we've had enough rain to last us for a while.

The Land We Borrow from Our Children
November 1, 2015

Our trees have played tricks on us this fall. Despite a number of frosty nights and cool days in early October, our soft maples and cottonwoods and locusts stayed uncharacteristically green, that is until just a few days ago. In my own quiet county, where hundreds of thousands of visitors come each year to enjoy red bridges and fall colors and the blind curves of rural gravel roads, our trees saved their best colors for the days after the tourists had headed home.

In just the last few days, and despite our brown grass and dusty air, what was once a sea of anemic green along our horizons has changed. Our woods now glow like backlit stained glass, their warm oranges and vivid yellows are alive in the slant of the evening sun.

We have loved this fall, my walking friend and I. She knows that I spend more and more time looking out of my desk-side window than writing by it when this time of year comes along, so on the weekends, and during our new and improved fall break from work, she agreed that we should walk a while in the woods, not only to see how the trees spent another year, but to exercise our legs on something other than asphalt. As explorers and hill climbers and branch waders we were as comfortable with one another as old shoes, and we sometimes had to push or pull one another up slopes that for some reason seemed steeper and longer this year than last.

We also decided to hike the gullies and washes of her parents' farm, rather than those in our own woods, for no reason in particular other than it had been a while since we had been there. Whereas we have an abundance of sycamores and wild cherry in ours, her old stomping grounds lean toward hickory and paw-paw and red oak. Despite an abundance of green there, we enjoyed seeing places we'd surely seen before, but it had been a few years, so much of our walk came to us as if we were there for the first time.

We have talked about building a house in those woods, but since it has taken us most of the last 35 years to get our own place in decent shape, we realize that construction of a dream home may still be just that, a dream. We walked up steep hillsides to an old field road that she often drove by tractor when she was a farm hand drafted by a father who had put several of his girls to work, for he had no sons. I could tell that Joanie, who is normally quiet anyway, was only partially with me for the hike, for I think she was reliving a bit of her childhood with each step, particularly when we reached the fields she'd worked nearly a lifetime ago. I didn't mind sharing the day with her memories, because I had a few of my own to run through too.

In all, we spent most of an afternoon in the

woods, searching for a long-lost graveyard that we never found, and exploring the old silo that was built long before her parents bought the farm over 60 years ago. We walked the branch that bi-sects the property, long dry, now just a meandering bit of sand that bends back on itself in many places; our kids played in that stream a thousand times. A hillside spring was still running, despite the dry weather, but we never found the spot where her dad had sunk a tile and run a line down to their old barn. In dry years, he'd push water up the hill to their house, because his four daughters and his wife often ran his shallow well dry.

I expect that more than anything else, Joanie and I spent our time re-convincing ourselves that the patch of woods we walked needs to be kept, that it would be a shame to see it logged or carved into smaller developed patches. More than once, a few words from Wendell Berry ran through my head, although I had to be home in front of a keyboard to get them exactly right.

He said we should be like "…a man who knows that the world is not given by his fathers, but borrowed from his children; who has undertaken to cherish it and do it no damage, not because he is duty-bound, but because he loves the world and loves his children."

I might add "grandchildren" to those words, for we have a grandson now, as well as a whole cast of grandnephews and nieces. I can't imagine them not having a place to explore, a place where they can breathe, just like the home ground we were fortunate to have. In this country, we are capable of giving our children and grandchildren a lot of things, but nothing should be more important to them than the gift of wild places.

That thought has been with me in the days since our walk. I continued to carry it in my head as I stepped along the banks of the Big Raccoon last week, as I wandered a little hilltop cemetery a few miles down the road one Sunday afternoon, and as I've watched the combines cutting the corn and beans that grew around us, transforming our fall landscape in the process.

The fall has come, and much of it is already gone. We need to treasure what is left of it.

The Great Squirrel Frenzy of 2016

February 1, 2016

As much as it sounds like I've gotten my hands on a bad movie script, I could hardly believe what I read last week while doing research for this story: More than once, Indiana has been invaded by marauding hordes of ravenous squirrels. I'm not kidding. That fact in itself may not be newsworthy this morning as you eat your cereal, but I certainly had no trouble taking it as truth after I looked out my kitchen window recently.

For me, winter Saturday mornings are spent with a coffee cup in one hand and a newspaper in the other, that is until I take to watching the birds. One of the first things I do nearly every morning—whether the sun is out of bed or not—is fill our feeders, usually with a generous scoop and two plastic cottage cheese containers overflowing with sunflower seeds, cracked corn, millet, and milo. I've been known to add a twist of suet and a few ears of corn to the mix, too.

Over the years, particularly since I've thrown in a thistle feeder for the chickadees and nuthatches and goldfinches, we've become an automat of sorts for a nice variety of birds, including blue jays and cardinals, and three kinds of woodpeckers: downy, red-bellied, and red-headed. We enjoy watching them spat with and out-maneuver one another for prizes, although they occasionally share a meal without bickering.

But we've also become a haven for squirrels, so many now that I'm beginning to fear we're soon going to be overrun, as Indiana was in 1811 (as a territory), 1822, 1826, and 1845.

I'm not going to complain too much about our furry-tailed friends; we actually invited them to the table a few years ago by hanging an ear corn feeder on a hulking wild cherry tree behind our barn. But we rarely saw the feeder used, its wares left impaled on a nail for weeks at a time with hardly a kernel gone missing.

Last summer, however, we began to notice more and more squirrels on our feeders in front of the house. Not exactly into sharing, they'd greedily sit on their haunches and gobble our seeds for hours, sometimes ignoring, but often harassing the birds who came to feed. It seemed as though the jays and bigger woodpeckers were the only birds willing to stand up to these thugs. Now, it's as if we've all given in to this gang of hoodlums who have ridden into town to terrorize innocent citizens.

As the warm days turned cool last fall, we began to notice that the fox squirrels we'd almost exclusively seen were vying for space with smaller grays. The latter seem to be more fidgety, more manic than their larger kin, so eventually we saw a segregation of sorts begin to take place: the fox squirrels harassing the more petite sparrows and wrens and cardinals at our small hanging feeder, and the gray squirrels duking it out with the larger birds on a platform feeder I have nailed to a maple tree.

There are four kinds of squirrels in Indiana. Besides the two I've already mentioned, flying squirrels and red squirrels—although not as common—can also be found, although I have never seen either on my place.

The gray squirrels (Sciurus carolinses) we see are early risers, often out of their warm beds and eating before dawn; then it's back to the sack until a late afternoon snack. Grays tend to be very active and alert, just one reason, I suppose, why they are smaller energy-burners, unlike the larger, heavier fox squirrels (Sciurus niger). Grays, like fox squirrels, also have notoriously bad memories; they rarely remember where they've left caches of food, often simply stumbling across the nuts and acorns that others have buried.

Of course, squirrels can be pests in more ways than one. Luckily, none have been able to find a way into my attic, which I understand is a nightmare along the line of demon possession. Because they crave salt, they tend to like wire insulation and the glue in plywood, appetites that prove to be real headaches for homeowners. Despite having as many as a dozen squirrels at our feeder at once, I have yet to see one anywhere near my roof.

As to the squirrel invasions of historic proportions, I turned to two online articles by David Heighway (Hamilton County) and Harold Morgan (Evansville) for more information. Heighway says that the "enormous waves of squirrels that swept across the United States … were as much a concern at that time as locust or disease." He noted that masses of squirrels were seen swimming across the White River, and that one Indianapolis businessman—Calvin Fletcher—claimed to have shot 284 of them in just three days in February 1823 around just one of his cornfields. He notes that one massive squirrel emigration in 1842 swept from Iowa to Wisconsin, leaving a path of gnawed destruction 130 miles wide and 150 miles long.

Morgan says the strange year of 1811 saw a squirrel migration that may have been connected to the sighting of a great twin-tailed comet, a solar eclipse, and hundreds of earthquakes along the New Madrid fault, including one quake that may have been among the greatest in history. In the fall of that year, it was said that squirrels lost their fear of people and acted strangely (dare I say they acted squirrelly?) and headed in massive numbers from north to south in what was yet to be called a state.

Anyway, I can't claim our population explosion of squirrels is on a Biblical scale just yet, and I don't think it's associated with impending earthquakes or comets, either. But, just in case, I'm buying an extra 100 pounds of birdseed this week.

Confessions of an Aluminum Can Junkie

March 14, 2016

Our garage, already cluttered with the overflow of the typical American consumer family that we are, is also stuffed with bags of soup cans, boxes of yellowing newsprint, flattened cardboard, and mountains of plastic.

We have even more stashed in the barn, ready to be loaded onto our pick-up truck for a trip over spring break into town to the recycling center.

Joanie and I have rinsed and sorted and crushed and bagged our refuse for years now, hoping, not for a chance to appear in a documentary about hoarders, but that we will have done our fair share for our grandchildren. We don't want them to have to live in a world where they drown in the garbage of their grandparents' generation, but we're not encouraged by what we see.

We have always recycled, and we're proud to say our children do it too. But when we began to pick up the roadside trash we found along our daily walks, we realized that much of what we were bagging needed to be recycled, particularly the aluminum beer and soda cans that we were finding in prodigious numbers.

It soon became clear, however, that our part-time diversion was becoming more of a full-time obsession, particularly for me. I am now a self-professed aluminum junkie, picking up squashed cans in store parking lots, jumping out of the car at lonely 4-way stops to grab the treasure I've spied in the ditches, and scanning the shoulders as we drive into town. "Can!" I'll inadvertently shout out, startling Joanie in mid-conversation, or jolting her awake from a nap. It's an uncontrollable reflex action; I may even be mumbling about them in my sleep now, and I hope I don't make friends self-conscious as I watch what they do with their empties.

Just a few days ago we attended a surprise birthday party for a high school friend of mine, and I have to admit that although I had a great time chatting with old buddies, and denying the stories they were telling, I kept my eye on a trash bin that sat nearby. It was filled with aluminum cans of all sorts, their siren song begging me to scoop them up and take them home for that first step toward recycling and rebirth. Only the stigma of being labeled either loony or needy kept me from picking out the cans that lay on top of the trash and discreetly slipping them out to the car. "Did you see all those cans in the trash?" Joanie asked me on the way home; she kind of has the bug, too…

Before you think we are merely trying to make a

buck, and that we are ignoring all other trash for the sake of taking aluminum only, hang on for the rest of the story: we pick up just about everything we can handle on our walking trips along the roads, sometimes dragging or juggling our finds a good distance home. But only on rare occasions do we see much of anything that has value—a tarp strap that has jiggled loose, a wrench that has fallen from a toolbox, an odd bolt here, perhaps a bent penny or scratched dime there. I found a perfectly good electrical outlet cover, still in its package, just a few days ago.

Aluminum cans do bring cash, but not much. They are 100 percent recyclable—every single atom of them is reusable—and Joanie and I can stuff about 50 into a single plastic grocery bag (which should, themselves, be banned, regardless of what many of our state legislators believe), but aluminum is actually the least-expensive metal per pound that is recycled. We're obviously not in it for the money, for as far as I can tell, it takes about 33 cans, give or take, to constitute a pound, and that brings—if we are lucky and the market isn't down—which it normally is—about a quarter. That's a lot of stooping and can crushing for 25 cents, a pay-off I would have been happy to get when I was 9 years old and Hershey Bars were a nickel.

I went in search of aluminum can data and came away with a ton of facts, most of which make me feel better about our recycling efforts. For instance, not long after our aluminum cans go to a recycler, they make their way back to a manufacturer where they are sorted and washed, undergo a re-melting process that removes all inks and dyes, and then are formed into ingots (each has the aluminum of about 1.6 million cans in it). The recycled metal is rolled into massive sheets, which are most often turned back into cans. The aluminum in the cans we are picking up today could be on a convenience store shelf in as little as six weeks. Most cans you may take a sip out of are made of about 70 percent recycled aluminum.

According to the Aluminum Association, a ton of recycled cans (I don't think we've picked up that many yet) can save 14,000 kilowatts of electricity, over 1,600 gallons of oil, and 10 cubic yards of landfill space (it takes 200-500 years for a single can to degrade); recycling one can saves enough energy to run a television for three hours, which is enough time for a few people I know to empty even more cans. With years of can-picking experience behind me, it is hard to believe that 120,000 aluminum cans are recycled every minute in this country; it obviously needs to be even more.

I still recall a great-uncle who was a prodigious beer drinker; none of his brew came in aluminum, despite the fact that the very first cans were pioneered by a beer manufacturer: Coors, in 1959. Royal Crown Cola began packaging its popular colas in cans first, in 1964. It was Ermal Cleon Fraze who helped the industry along by inventing the aluminum tab for opening the cans, while Daniel Cudzik, a Reynolds Aluminum employee, devised the stay-on tab in 1975.

Right now, anyway, my friends are enabling my addiction to aluminum. Several of our school's teachers and custodians save their empties for me; I keep them in a bag in my room to bring home each Friday, and it's with great satisfaction that their empties join what we've gleaned along the roads. We don't drink much more than water in our house, so virtually every can we recycle comes to us from somewhere else.

Not long before my grandson was born, Joanie and I decided that whatever amount of money we made when we cashed in our aluminum cans was going into his college savings account; if he's lucky, we'll have enough saved for a few textbooks.

It's nearly spring, and I'm hopeful that those who drive in my end of the county with their windows down will hang on to their trash a while longer and dispose of it at home. But if they don't, I hope it's aluminum cans they toss out the window.

A Month for Warmth and Woods and Words
April 25, 2016

Just as I suspected, April has done what it is known to do more often than not. In a matter of just a day or two, I have gone from the comfort of an extra blanket on the bed to the feel of sweat trickling down my back as I stoop to pull a few weeds.

It is a Jekyll and Hyde month, April is, but I love it despite its moodiness. Mark Twain was not speaking of an Indiana spring when he said that he had "experienced 136 kinds of weather in 24 hours," but it certainly applies to us.

My woods have reflected the month's temperament. Slow to bloom and bud in April's early cool weeks, it is now abuzz with activity.

Of course, I can't stay out of the woods when I see the trillium and redbuds so busy making themselves known, so last Saturday, despite a list of chores as long as my leg, I walked across the yard and into the woods with my son. He had come to call with our grandson, and while Joanie got the little guy lunch, Evan and I headed across the greening briars of a fence row into the woods.

If a mushroom was to show up at my feet, I'd have availed myself to nab it, but although my son was searching—with little success—for morels, I was content to just walk among the trees, favorite hiking staff in hand, taking in what I can't get anywhere else: a nature fix, of sorts.

The cold of earlier nights has had no effect on the woodland phlox and spring beauties that carpet some places in our woods, for even though our hilly property is yet to look as it will in just another week or two—especially if we get a little rain—I found myself walking into patches of lavender and white which rivaled that found in calendar photos. It made me happy, not just to own land, but to have the privilege of wandering about on it.

How anyone, even with the cares of the world on his shoulders, could not feel better after seeing what I was seeing is beyond my comprehension.

Of course, before I began this account, I had planned to write a story about it being National Poetry Month; after all, I had promised to do so earlier in April when I wrote in praise of the virtues of libraries, and librarians, and everything good related to reading. And so, that I will do.

Although I could find no exact reason why April was chosen, National Poetry Month was first suggested by the Academy of American Poets in 1995, and the month-long celebration became a reality the next year. I'd like to think that the AAP opted for April because it is, at least in my opinion, a month that has so much to offer, including inspiration for renewal and optimism, beauty and nature.

Poetry, like so many other things, used to be more important to us, and I don't mean just cranky old English teachers who drone on about the significance of Gerald Manley Hopkins while students screenshoot their literature homework. I mean average, everyday citizens: housewives and construction workers, bank tellers and sales clerks. Americans grew up with poetry, learned to read it through the Scriptures, memorized it in schools, even read it daily in newspapers and magazines. More Americans respected, even revered, poets years ago, and I'm not quite sure when it ceased to be so important to us. If I remember correctly, Henry Longfellow and John Greenleaf Whittier's birthdays were considered to be so significant, that for a time, schoolchildren were given days off to celebrate. I have opened scrapbooks of poetry clipped from newspapers, seen dozens of poems kept for posterity and remembrance in Bibles and dictionaries and novels, all yellowed and hidden from view for generations.

Although I am not advocating a National Sylvia Plath Day or the like, I will say that schools need to teach more poetry, and it would be nice if state academic standards allowed for more of it. A stanza or two of poetry might show up on an end-of-course assessment on occasion, but poetry isn't considered a priority anymore. I sure hope there are a lot of teachers out there who are teaching poetry despite the discouraging directives, and it is too bad that they have to justify teaching the beauty and wisdom of Whitman and Yeats and Teasdale to children. Surely, as a nation, we have enough intelligence and education to produce great industries, innovative technologies, and advanced medicine, yet still encourage a few budding poets, too.

Years ago, far more print space was used in newspapers for poetry. Some of it was locally produced, and much of it was poorly written, but 19th century newspapers often reserved front page space for poems. Can you imagine that now? Since, proportionally, more Americans in those days read newspapers, more were probably reading poetry, too. I imagine very few literate households did not have a book of poetry in it; even almanacs carried verse. I can't prove it, but I feel we are better for reading poetry; it is another one of those things that helps us hang on to our humanity and compassion and perspective.

I wanted to close this story with a poem about spring, so I turned to my window to think a bit about a few lines that would be appropriate. But somewhere between Robert Frost and Linda Pastan, I got to watching a bumblebee—the first I've seen this spring—as he bobbed and wove along my cabin railing before heading down to the wood line to take a look at a patch of lunaria growing there. A minute or two later, my daughter dropped in to announce that she and her mother were taking a walk, and I was to unsaddle from my desk chair and get out into the sun with them.

While they talked and walked, I loped ahead with my own thoughts. Along the way I heard—both coming and going—the song of a mockingbird, its beautiful solo much louder than a whole chorus of blackbirds and robins and killdeer.

I knew then that I didn't need to think of a poem at all; the green of April, its birdsong and blue skies, its purple irises and lilac blooms, are poetry. It is, after all, the month for it.

Splendor of the Butterweed Plowed Under

June 6, 2016

I know that I will irritate my farmer friends when I say it, but I hated to see the butterweed disappear under their plows last week. Our rainy spring has dissolved in a bubble of dry summer air these past few days, and with the absorbent warmth came the tardy tractors that have been running nearly non-stop to get seed in the ground.

For a number of wet weeks, I enjoyed seeing the brilliant yellow of the weed as it grew in the damp fields, its dramatic color in contrast to the green of the woods and a sometimes-blue sky. So what is undoubtedly an aggravation to those who make a living trying to grow corn and soybeans has been pleasing to me, and I apologize for that pleasure. But I knew it would be gone soon enough.

It isn't practical to grow weeds on farm ground for aesthetic reasons, and now that I have watched acres of the stuff tilled under, I know that it will be replaced in just a week or two by neatly placed rows of emerging seedlings.

Butterweed is actually called cressleaf groundsel; it is not wild mustard, as some folks believe, but rather a member of the daisy and aster family. I asked one of my wife's farmer cousins what he called the plant, and he told me that it is sometimes named "yellow rocket," and added, "It can be a real problem if you let it go to seed, because it puts out heads something like a dandelion, and that fluff clogs up air filters and radiators."

In no way is my story today an indictment of impersonal technology as it invades the delicate balance of nature. I'm happy to see the farmers working the fields now; when they aren't, I miss seeing them as they put things in order, mowing near the fences, working to drain fields by digging ditches and laying in plastic lines, walking out among the growing plants to check the progress of their crops.

But I always wonder about what we lose when we tame the land. Just last evening, Joanie and I walked our walk, later than we have had to for months since it was quite warm. Along the way, we passed a pretty patch of pasture, overgrown already with tall orchard grass that was blowing in the breeze.

"They'll be mowing that soon," I said as I nodded to the south. "It will be the first cutting of grass hay we've seen," she added, and both of us began to imagine what the place will look like after the grass is neatly mowed and the land is dotted with huge green bales. The sweet smell of them will be worth the sweat of walking past it all.

Yet, I also know that there will be a toll enacted by the tractors and balers. The occasional black snake will not escape the blades of the mowers, and rabbits and birds will either flee or die in the wake of the machinery's roar. What will have become of that acre's killdeer and voles, its butterflies and caterpillars, we will never know. There is no way to calculate just how much havoc will be wrought upon the land's unfortunate inhabitants.

We have also been watching a hilltop forest on our way to church each Sunday, and we've seen the loggers' trucks and dozers parked for the weekend near the mouths of muddy impromptu roads. I know we need lumber and pulp wood—after all, I write for a newspaper—but I can't help but wonder what disaster the trucks and saws and heavy equipment wreak on the inhabitants of that land. What becomes of the box turtles and squirrels that live there? What of the foxes and owls and raccoons?

So too then, there is a cost when the plows get moving, and I understand that has to happen, but I also think of the field mice—who I hope have no intentions of panhandling at my house—and where they are expected to go. I see them a bit like poet Ted Kooser, who wrote in his poem, "Spring Plowing," that the mice were like refugees from a war, relocating to the higher ground of the fence rows, the wheels of their tiny carts squeaking in the grass.

Not far from the pasture I spoke of, we also caught the strong scent of a stand of honeysuckle that has overwhelmed an old set of corner posts where a fence once ran along the road. I suppose it should be eradicated, for it is an invasive species that has the potential to overtake an entire woods. But I have a tendency to leave alone that which does me no harm, and with luck we'll be smelling its aroma for years to come.

Until next spring, I will just have to miss looking out across the fields of butterweed, but I look forward to the deep green of the corn that will soon take its place.

Up a Creek with a Paddle

July 24, 2016

Big Raccoon Creek is part of a watershed that drains about 215 square miles and originates as a trickle in Montgomery County; it then picks up steam south of a great lake the Army Corps of Engineers built nearly 60 years ago and meanders through the southern half of Parke County. Flatboats were built on it, corn has been ground at mills beside it, and the county's first seat of government sat near it. My wife and I just borrow it every once in a while.

It should be in no way misconstrued that a "mid-life" crisis led Joanie and me to buy kayaks early this spring to paddle the Big Raccoon. We have no intention of searching for white water challenges; can't be considered candidates for reality adventure programs; won't be appearing in AARP's magazine as examples of "active seniors" anytime soon. Simply put, we want to keep moving as we age, and besides our daily walks, could think of no better way to do it—while reliving a bit of our childhoods at the same time—than on nearby creeks. The Big Raccoon is not only closest to us, it is a part of us.

If you have read much of what I write, then you know that we both grew up in the country, roaming farm fields and exploring the woods; we have never lived in a town. We wanted and provided the same for our children, and want it even more for our grandchildren. American kids, even those who live in the country, are losing touch with their natural roots—with playing in the dirt and climbing trees and wading creeks—and it frightens us.

Several times now we have put ourselves onto the Big Raccoon, a stream that wanders about like a Bedouin. It is often a brown and muddy creek, a bit erratic as countless branches and the lake's overflow drain into it, so we have chosen our spots, hiking to the Roseville Bridge to check the water's height and clarity before we get on it. We plan to head to other streams, perhaps a lake or two, as we get more experience with our boats.

We are not rookies with paddles; both of us spent time in canoes as kids, and we were seasoned veterans at wading and swimming, sandbar inspecting and rock picking by the time we started grade school. I camped along Spring Creek and the Big Raccoon with regularity until I was in college, fished and seined them both with my grandfather; Joanie plowed fields that bordered the creek to the east, so it was never very far from her reach either. So returning to the creeks to experience their feels and smells were familiar sensations for us. We have not spent enough time there in recent years, precious little since our kids have grown and made lives for themselves.

The story of how we got our particular kayaks is an interesting one too: Not long after I wrote a December column about our lack of Christmas gift ideas—which included an aside about kayaks—Deb McKinney contacted me to let me know that she and her husband, Larry, had enjoyed kayaking for years.

After Larry died last fall, Deb knew she couldn't enjoy her boats like she used to, so she offered them to us, not to make an investment back, but because she hoped we would enjoy them as much as she and Larry had.

We bought them in March, and I could tell the day we picked them up that it wasn't easy for Deb. As we loaded them, I believe she could still picture her husband fishing Sugar Creek with their son, or the two of them relaxing on Rockville Lake together. I want to assure her now that the kayaks are still supplying plenty of enjoyment, and will for years to come.

Our trips down the Big Raccoon—an ironic statement since it ambles to the north most of the way that we're on it—have mostly been exercises in peace and quiet. Not long after we put in near Rosedale for the first time, I couldn't help but remember something Thoreau wrote in his *A Week on the Concord and Merrimack Rivers*, an account he published 10 years after a canoe trip he took with his brother, John, in 1839. I have never finished the book, but I recall that Thoreau said in it that it is a tragedy that people often don't understand silence.

Of course, it is never completely quiet as we kayak, and there is much to see: a water snake that Joanie spotted as it sunned on a barkless tree trunk; a deer that barged out of a cornfield, only to catch sight of me and backtrack; the restless flutter of cottonwood leaves in the wind.

We go with the flow of the creek, but still hear our paddles as they plop into the water to send a stroke swell of current beneath us. We hear, perhaps above all else, the birds that live alongside and over the stream. We regularly see eagles and hawks, herons and killdeer, crows and thrashers, but two other birds have come to fascinate us with their habits and voices too.

In places where the creek has widened itself into turns, and swirling water has cut steep inclines into surrounding fields, bank swallows turn the available space into condos; they restlessly flit about their estates waiting for us to pass them by. I could be wrong, but I suspect that they are a slightly different version of the swallows we've seen fly from adobe nests that are plastered under the concrete bridges that cross the creek. Just north of Rosedale, the Thorpe Ford Bridge, built in 1912 but closed to traffic 55 years ago, is used for sightseeing only now. The underpinnings of the modern bridge next to the old wooden structure attract the swallows.

The noisiest birds we hear and see are belted kingfishers. They are big-headed and ragged-crested and they rattle and squawk in their hyperactivity. Kingfishers never sit still, and have never allowed me to get a photo of them with the small waterproof camera I carry. They are a blur of blue and white and brown, and although I read that that they eat crayfish and minnows, I have never seen them do more than zip from one branch to another, always far enough around a bend to keep us from getting a good look at them.

We prefer that the water be fairly low when we kayak; we like it to be clear, and truth be told we often stop, not to rest, but to snoop along the large sandbars that dot the creek. The flotsam that is left in the gravel is a mixture of the natural and man-made. As we have done along the roads near our place, we have begun to collect trash that has been left in the creek, mostly aluminum soda and beer cans. I have picked up a few broken bottles too, and once found an ancient coffee pot, no doubt lost by a camper years ago.

I thought I had discovered a great treasure a few weeks back. At a point not far from where we put in, a pair of concrete bridge abutments from the old Vandalia Line sit as bookends on the creek's banks; the wooden railroad bridge between them is long gone. The water was low, and as I slid along the west bank, I saw what appeared to be a large wrench peeking up out of the water. I figured it had been dropped from a train at least a half-century ago, but when I waded over to pick it up, I found it anchored solid. I am still unsure what it is, but suspect that a cable was once fastened to it for some reason.

The sandbars are also the repository for gravel, for which I still have a childhood fascination. The creek has mostly a sandy or cool clay bottom, having a bit of a wind-blown look in places as the current shapes it eon after eon, but where the creek turns—and it does that drastically and often—the sand and rock build up and force the water to eventually go around. One of our favorite stops is such a place; it comes not long after Little Raccoon Creek ends its run from Jessup and points northeast to meet its big brother. Their confluence is an understated affair.

I spent hours as a boy picking up crinoids and conglomerates, bits of polished glass and quartz; I probably still would. I have re-appointed myself chief inspector of mussel shells, driftwood, and spider webs too. Just last week, Joanie and I watched a killdeer as she faked dire distress, all so we'd be led away from a nest she'd ill-advisedly built in the debris. In many ways, these shoals are as interesting to us as what flies overhead or swims beneath us.

Our voyages have not been long, and have hardly been arduous. In our first few trips we have had to push ourselves out of shallow spots but a few times and have yet to portage our kayaks around jams; it has been easy going by design, not work at all. We have noticed that for some reason the dragonflies—bigger than we see in our garden—like to hitch rides on our boats, having a special attraction for the reflective silver and blue emblems near the kayaks' cockpits. They land on us too, competing with the yellow and black swallowtails that have yet to buy tickets for our shoulders.

Lugging our kayaks up fairly steep banks for reloading seems to make us sweat more than anything else. We straddle poison ivy and try to get toeholds in the mud, and more than once I've had to let our boats slip back into the water—as if they know they belong there—so I can get a better grip or balance.

Even though we are only a third or so into the summer, the season is about to end for us; we return to school soon, and our time for kayaking will be gone. But we have gotten a taste of it in these past few months, and plan to go again soon, hopeful that each time we get a little better at pointing our kayaks in the right direction and that we can read the creek like a favorite book.

Just last week, I enjoyed a photo story in a year-old *Yankee* magazine. It was about a group of Thoreau scholars and tourism advocates who had completed a 325-mile canoe trip into the heart of Maine's wilderness; it took them over two weeks, and with considerable hardship they replicated a journey that Thoreau made in 1857 (just five years before he died of tuberculosis) with the help of a Penobscot Indian guide named Joe Polis.

I have doubts that I would make such a trip, even considering the waterproof tents and modern sleeping bags and expert guides the group had. Our little forays into the Indiana woods, never far from a road or cell service or town, are hardly trips into the Maine back country, yet they are enough to help us get reacquainted with our roots, both literal and figurative. Despite our wrinkles, we become children again, and a desire for seeing things for ourselves is renewed.

Craggy old John Burroughs may not have said it about my mate and me, but it applies to our paddling the Big Raccoon. "I go to nature to be soothed and healed, and to have my senses put in tune once more."

Cicadas Always Know the Time of Day

August 15, 2016

I walked out on my back deck near dark a few nights ago with nothing particular in mind except to have one last look around after a day of chores. As I heard the door's latch click behind me, I picked up on the sound of the cicadas singing high in the trees, just as they have for over a month now.

The "boisterous song" of the cicadas, typical of the natural world because it is a mating call, soon grew so loud and dissonant that it nearly hurt my ears. Yet cicadas seem to me to be the very essence of summer, as predictable as a horizon of corn, as comforting as a star-filled sky or a firefly-lit meadow. When we recall the Indiana summers of our childhoods, I suppose we include cicada-composed symphonies among the memories.

Cicadas are not locusts, although I remember my grandparents and cousins referring to them as such. What we hear each summer—more so in some years than in others—are annual cicadas (Tibicen carnicularis), not those that show up to great fanfare every 13 or 17 years, as if some Biblical plague was upon us.

This summer has been perfect for the annual variety, for it has been as steamy as a Turkish bath. Yet, the cicada is also a harbinger of the coming fall; early settlers called it the "Dog Days Harvest Fly," for as its song lessens, corn-picking can't be far off.

There is much speculation about cicadas. Most of us hear them, but they are rarely seen, spending virtually every moment of their lives as nymphs working like Welsh coal miners underground. When they do emerge—and there is little hard science that can tell us the why and when of the individual timing of that—they leave behind the brown crusty shells of their metamorphosis hanging on trees like translucent dinosaur skeletons, then head to the rarified atmosphere of the tree crown.

I remember walking around the corner of the house one summer day years ago to see one of our cats batting a cicada around on the sidewalk like a buzzing hockey puck, but there have been entire seasons that I have heard them only. By luck—knowing that I was going to write this story—I spotted one as it crept to the top of one of my backyard silver maples several days ago; it hesitated just long enough for me to take a picture.

On a few other occasions, I have seen them awkwardly and slowly bumbling around in the dusky air, and remember an instance years ago when one fell out of a tree onto my shoulder as I trimmed a nuisance limb. We went eyeball to eyeball for a minute before I brushed it off, slightly repulsed by something that looked as if it had come from a bad science fiction movie.

As I most often do when dealing with the bugs and beasts I encounter around my place, I consulted Allen Young's *Small Creatures and Ordinary Places*, a favorite book of nature essays. Of course, Allen included a chapter about our noisy friends, and just last year he sent a newspaper story he'd written about cicadas to me. I need to look no further for the facts; Young is the curator emeritus of zoology at the Milwaukee Public Museum.

As in so many other cases, Young fears that we hear cicadas less often than we used to for all the wrong reasons. The land, under which cicada nymphs live, tunneling and guzzling tree sap for nourishment, is being increasingly stressed by development and clearing. For every parking lot paved and housing development raised, there are going to be fewer cicadas.

Young reminds us that cicadas are indelibly linked to both our trees and seasons: "No one really knows for sure how a cicada nymph measures time and decides the fateful moments of pushing itself out of the earth and darkness, but it is surely a marvel of nature's precision," he writes. "Whatever nature uses to keep time, the cicadas 'hear.' The creature knows when to make its entrance and exit." He says that after years (it may be up to a decade) of digging around in the soil, a cicada's life above ground lasts only a few weeks—just long enough to get to the top of a tree, sing a bit, mate with the mute females, and leave eggs behind.

If fortune smiles on those eggs, enough that they avoid encounters with ants and birds and other hungry predators, they'll drop to the ground to start the whole process over again. Birds and raccoons, squirrels and cicada-killing wasps are all enemies of this awkward-looking, bulb-eyed creature for landing one means a considerable meal.

Cicadas remind me of how spoiled I am. When I was a boy, and air conditioning seemed to be reserved for the wealthy, I lived with the songs of cicadas well into the summer nights. With open and screened windows, we awoke to their sound all through our summer vacations, and only when they grew silent did we know for sure that autumn couldn't be far away.

Often, as I camped on some creek bank or in some clearing in the woods, most often too hot to be covered or to scoot very close to a fire, it was the drone of the cicadas that kept me awake well into the night or woke me in the morning.

It is a warm August morning as I write these recollections. My windows are open and most of what I hear, besides the light drone of a ceiling fan above me, are cicadas in the trees around me. It is said that they sing loudest when it is hot and humid and clear, so today is a good day for them. The forecasts I have seen assure prime singing weather ahead too.

I still know very little about cicadas, not much more than when I was a kid and I was picking their shells off the big beech trees that circled our yard. But to hear them reminds me of childhood and makes me appreciate how little I know about the life that surrounds me in the grass and trees. Most of us are guilty of that, I suppose.

"We know them like we know our own breath," Young writes. "… a constant presence about which we 'know' nothing at all."

The Grasshopper Is a Musician

September 26, 2016

Consider the lowly grasshopper: Celebrated in

children's books, light poetry and silly songs, they are also condemned as ravenous pillagers in both biblical scripture and pioneer history. Yet grasshoppers are ever-present voices and flashes of color among the sights and sounds of our summers. This year, perhaps more so.

I have been seeing more grasshoppers around my place these past few months, and I am inexplicably pleased. Just a few days ago, a teacher friend said the same thing.

For years, it seems to me, grasshoppers have not been nearly as noticeable. Yet through this summer—and now, into early fall—I have seen more of them hopping among my browning irises, clinging to my cabin's rails, hanging on the house's siding. I can't say that my flowers or shrubs look the worse for wear after enduring a grasshopper summer, for by this time of year, and despite plentiful rain, everything looks a bit weary and haggard. Three months of hot summer sun can do that, even when grasshopper populations are low.

I don't think it was because I spent just about every waking moment outdoors when I was a boy that helped me notice grasshoppers in those days; I really do think they were more plentiful then, and I have no doubt that our wholesale destruction of natural habitats and the overuse of pesticides are now contributors to that.

However, grasshoppers, which can also be called locusts—for the names are interchangeable—would present us with catastrophe had modern science and farmers not checked their numbers with chemicals. They would, literally, eat us out of house and home.

Tom Turpin, Ph.D., a professor of entomology in Purdue's College of Agriculture, tells me he isn't sure I am seeing more grasshoppers around my yard this year, unless I am simply looking for them.

"It is likely that you saw more grasshoppers when you were a kid because, in general, you might also have paid closer attention at the time," he said. My grade school teachers would have argued mightily with that determination.

Turpin did say that "less predation on [grasshopper] egg masses over winter, less disease in young grasshoppers after the hatch, or good winter survival [for the eggs]" are likely reasons that I am seeing more hoppers in my yard. But I really have no factual explanation for their presence. In some past summers, I have hardly seen them; this year, they are everywhere, including a few that have met an unfortunate end with the grill of my truck.

I have written plenty about grasshoppers' cricket cousins in past stories, for their late summer screeching—particularly if one manages to get into the house—drives me to distraction. Grasshoppers are noise makers too. As a matter of fact, according to insect expert Debbie Hadley, grasshoppers make noises in two ways: stridulation and crepitation.

The former term means grasshoppers simply rub their hind legs against a forewing; tiny sharp "pegs" on the inside of the legs catch the thickened edge of the wings. It is not wholly unlike someone wearing a pair of whale-ribbed corduroy pants for a brisk walk. Some grasshoppers, however, crepitate—well, those built for it, anyway—by loudly snapping their wings as they fly.

In her article, "10 Fascinating Facts about Grasshoppers," Hadley also mentions that grasshoppers continue to wreak havoc in some regions, particularly on grazing grounds that aren't normally sprayed with pesticides. She also mentions that in many areas of Asia and Africa, people use grasshoppers as a staple source of protein in their diets; she even mentions John the Baptist, who ate locusts and honey, as described in the third chapter of Matthew. Having accidentally smashed too many crickets in my darkened garage over the years, I have no interest whatsoever in making their close relatives a meal anytime soon.

To look at a grasshopper up close, under a magnifying glass, for instance, is a fascinating thing. Armor-plated like prehistoric dinosaurs, tank-like grasshoppers are built for battle, and, in fact, can be quite aggressive, despite their avuncular and innocent appearance. Hadley says that grasshoppers' ancestors actually developed 200-300 million years ago, and I have to believe that had I been alive then, grasshoppers would have been eating me instead of the other way around. Just a few weeks ago, I saw a large hopper on one of my potted plants. I grabbed him in a quick slight of hand only to have him bite me on a finger.

It may be kids' stuff, but my crash course on grasshoppers these past few days has been fun. In some ways, I am reminded of my time watching "Dr. Hopp and Friends" on afternoon television. Aesop may have been right in depicting grasshoppers as lazy when compared to the industrious ant, but I find them interesting, nonetheless. I prefer Roald Dahl's take in *James and the Giant Peach,* for in it, the old green grasshopper simply says, "I have never been a pest in my life. I am a musician."

Perhaps, Dr. Turpin is right. Maybe I am seeing more grasshoppers because I am looking for them, for I am reminded of something else Dahl's grasshopper also says: "There are a whole lot of things in this world of ours you haven't started wondering about yet."

October's Different Slant of Light

October 24, 2016

We saw our neighbors stacking firewood on their front porch a few nights ago. It was warm, and Joanie and I were out for a walk in the shorts and T-shirts we'd thought we'd seen the last of for a while.

But Drew and Shirley Yando were warmer than we were, their foreheads glistening in the sun, their shirts sticking to their backs as they tossed the wood out of the back of their pick-up truck. I think Drew wanted us to stop and chat just so he could rest a bit, but Shirley looked as if she just wanted to get the job done and sit down. It was getting late, and we hadn't had our supper yet, so we kept putting one foot in front of the other.

A heavy rain earlier in the day had left enough water on the road to create a steam bath of sorts for us, and the sun, although dropping toward a cornfield to our west, was still heating us up enough that we were glad to see a cool dark tunnel of trees ahead on our way north to the Roseville Bridge.

If we hadn't seen so many leaves that had already changed their clothes to fall colors—or had to keep our eyes open for Covered Bridge Festival traffic—we could have sworn it was mid-summer.

But it is fall, and our warm days are nearly gone. The breeze, stoked hot and from the south yet today, is to come out of the north later in the week, so we had better enjoy it while we can. The Yandos' chores were just one sign that winter isn't that far off. More and more I see other "neighbors" putting things up for fall so they can make it through the winter.

For instance, a young deer, not far past still having its belly speckled, has been grazing these last few weeks under a shingle oak just north of our house. He's never more than a few yards from the woods and escape, but he's there in the early evenings, munching, I suppose on the acorns that have been falling in the breeze. When the acorns are gone, I imagine he might move even closer to the house and another oak. That is, if the squirrels leave him anything to eat.

We've heard tree frogs peeping here and there, particularly when we walk past the wet woods and creek bottoms. It is a bit unusual to hear them in October, but I don't think they have been fooled into thinking it is summer again. A little rain and warm, steamy weather can't fool their onboard biological time clocks.

We just imagine they were out looking for a little romance before spending their winter in cold lonely leaf beds. A few nights in the 40s will surely curb their enthusiasm, but I hope I continue to hear them in the evenings through my screens, until I get too cool to keep my windows open.

As we neared the bridge a few minutes after seeing the Yandos, I caught a glimpse of a big groundhog as he blasted through a brush-choked gulley. Our voices had startled him, but he still had managed to nab something from around the dumpster that sits near the Rock Run Café and Bakery; it was a hamburger bun, I think.

I have never gotten the impression that groundhogs are judicious hoarders of food, so I imagine he didn't run far before he gobbled his prize. It is my understanding that groundhogs don't really hibernate, but go through extended periods of light sleep a dozen or so times through the winter. They surely have a few snacks on hand when they wake up, for I have never seen a slim one.

Everywhere along our walk we saw signs of autumn. The hard rain had meant we'd see no combines raising dust off in the distance, but we did think the cornfields along the way looked dowdy, many of the stalks already snapped under the weight of their drying ears of corn. The building breezes rattled the sandpapery leaves, and as I have often said in this space, it is a pleasant sound to me.

We saw a stand of sassafras ablaze in orange, a fence row filled with the fading yellow leaves and outrageously red berries of honeysuckle, and a stand of bright red poison ivy that grew up the trunk of a pair of locust trees along our property. It was at the height of its glory—the only time I look forward to seeing its wicked leaves, but it will soon fade to a dull purple before dropping its load like everything else.

It doesn't just take a glance through my windows down into the woods to know that fall is here, that I have much to do before the first snow flies. The wind chimes we have on our porches have been ringing loud and clear this week, the wind out of the south and west as if it were summer. But soon they'll change their tunes as the breeze shifts from the north.

As for me, I have already been raking leaves and trimming the dregs of our flower gardens away. Today, I have a few dead limbs to cut up, and I want to clean our bird boxes. I will work to pick up the fallen and dried and blown for weeks to come.

Our birds sense the change that is coming. Just last week, I caught sight of a northern flicker, a big woodpecker-like bird with a flash of yellow under its wings, as it picked away on the ground, for ants and beetles.

My bird guide tells me that they live here year-round, but I have only seen them in the fall. The blue jays are back now too, the hummingbirds gone, and I have had some thoughtful minutes watching our skittish gold finches tug on the heads of the spent coneflowers that surround my cabin. Soon, they'll go back to our thistle feeder, but they favor those needle-like seeds right now; they can have the thistle all winter if they like.

Perhaps most of all, I am noticing the slant of the sunlight changing, particularly in the evening as we walk. On the night we headed for the bridge, I saw shafts of misty sunlight cutting through the limbs of the trees that grow along a branch that empties into the Big Raccoon. I don't see the sun just like that all summer.

Poet Emily Dickinson wrote of a "certain slant of light," but she was speaking of winter afternoons in her poem. I think I know what she meant, and October is still with us.

A Resolution I Intend to Keep

January 2, 2017

I have never been much of a resolution maker. I try to shed a few pounds when my pants feel too tight, get off the couch when I feel I've sat too long, listen to a little Aaron Copland or the breeze in my wind chimes when I feel the din of American pop culture rattling in my skull.

But after reading an article in a late December issue of *The Week* a few days ago, I do hereby resolve to spend more time in this new year outdoors; it will be good for me.

Found in the health and science section, the piece listed several things that researchers have pretty well proven to be good for us; happily, books, dirt, and carbohydrates are among them.

Included in the few paragraphs about the benefits of exercise was this statement: "...another study found that people who do the equivalent of about two and a half hours of walking a week have a lower risk of about 13 different forms of cancer."

The article also suggested that exercising—and I do that outside in the form of yard work and walking our roadsides and hiking the woods, not in a gym on a treadmill—is also a proven factor in fighting "cognitive decline."

I have always believed that a good injection of nature is a cure-all for many of our problems. I don't think I can recall a single instance when I haven't felt better—both mentally and physically—after putting a few rural miles on my bony old feet.

Interestingly, exercise's benefits may actually increase when we sweat outside in fresh air amongst green things, that news reported in a *Washington Post* story written by Chelsea Harvey last April.

Titled, "Why living around nature could make you live longer," Harvey's article draws data from a number of interesting studies, including one from Harvard University, funded by the National Institute on Health. The study actually used satellite images that determined how much vegetation surrounded the participant's homes, and it determined that "people living in the greenest places...had a 12 percent lower rate of mortality from any non-accidental cause than people who lived in the least greenest places."

I know my love—my need—for green places is in my DNA. Country-raised, I can dip my toes into the waters of urban life and city traffic only so long before I have to head home. I once told a friend of mine who left our mostly rural county several years ago to live in a very nice, but crowded suburban neighborhood, that Joanie and I considered moving only farther out into the country if we ever decided to relocate, although we know that our age may someday dictate just the opposite. We need the sound of wind blowing through trees like we need food; we own a car if and when we need to drive into a town. I don't want to look at pictures of birds and creeks and fields just on my computer screen or through a car window; I want to see them and hear them and live with them.

It appears now, too, according to Harvey's article, that science is also verifying the positive effects of country living on our mental health as well. The Dean of the School of Public Health at the University of Washington, Howard Frumkin, is a proponent of famed naturalist E.O. Wilson's "biophilia hypothesis." Wilson believed that our connection to nature is embedded in our genetic composition. "Something about contact with nature is soothing and restorative and thereby good for mental health," Frumkin says.

I can verify that; my family's idea of a vacation

may sound frumpy and boring to some, but it has to come in the form of a forest or beach or mountain view; I have to admit that I'd rather take a beating than go to an amusement park or spend more than an hour at a shopping mall. Just the other day, as I struggled to come up with an idea for this very story, my wife suggested that I bundle up against the cold and take a walk. "Something will come to you, if you don't freeze first," she said.

I know the argument I've presented for this daily dose of nature may be a shallow one; I simply know it works for me. Although I tend to avoid the things the magazine listed as bad for us—opioids, distracted walking (I don't pack a cell phone when I head out), alcohol, and trampolines, for example—I am a notoriously fitful sleeper, and insomnia, according to the article, is a huge detriment to one's health. But in the year ahead, I hope I can push myself away from a desk more often to head outside; perhaps I'll sleep a little better for it too.

Frumkin added: "If we had a medication that … prolonged life, that addressed very different unconnected causes of disease, that did it at no cost and with no side effects, that would be the best medication of the decade. But we don't have a medication like that except for this 'vitamin N'—nature."

There is an old Creole proverb that reads: "The crow may be caged, but his thoughts are in the field." Perhaps in the year ahead, this old crow can get out of his cage more often.

On the Color of January Days
January 30, 2017

I have been a bit glum as I've glanced out of my window this month to see the wind moving our maple trees' stark branches, a gunmetal sky serving as backdrop, my yard dotted with pools of rainwater.

Winter seems to be getting harder for Joanie and me to bear. Although cold weather in itself isn't that much of a bother, we have grown to dislike the grim, leaden days and long nights of January and February. It seems as though the color has been bleached from the landscape, that is until I look at our bird feeders and tree tops, which are alive with woodpeckers and blue jays and juncos.

Joanie and I feed the birds out of habit and interest, perhaps with a bit of sympathy thrown in. Neither of us can comprehend how animals in the wild, particularly those dabs of feathers and feet, can survive a winter on their own. Just the other morning, I walked out to my cabin, a cup of coffee in hand, ready to work on a feature story, and as I glanced down into the woods, I saw three young deer huddled together in the leaves, no more than 50 yards away from my back door. It was a bitterly cold day, hardly out of the single digits, and I shivered just thinking about spending a night outdoors as they just had. Nimble and quick and nearly delicate, they are resiliently tough.

This winter's temperatures have been a pleasant surprise, one that my gas supplier probably resents but my wallet appreciates. It has also been one filled, so far, with day after day of drab, mousy weather. It has rained more than snowed, and I have driven to work in early-morning fog for most of the past few weeks. Our birds, however, step up to our sunflower seed snack bar regularly, that is when our squirrels don't scare them away.

We have an abundance of squirrels, both fox and gray, and as long as they don't invade my attic, they can stick around. However, the seed we leave is mostly for our birds, for they can't hide food in burrows or nests like squirrels; they need it nearly round-the-clock to keep their hammering little hearts going. Of course, like the deer, they are tougher than they look, and often spend most of their time around the feeders squawking and picking away at each other rather than eating. There seems to be little cooperation among them, although I do believe I have seen the goofy little nuthatches keeping the squirrels occupied on one side of the feeder while a raid is conducted on the other.

I am encouraged by the color of the birds. The flashes of red from our cardinals come in stark contrast to the brown grass or white snow. We have a magnolia tree in our front yard, and I often see them there, segregating themselves like private club members among the willowed tips of the tree's branches. They are easily frightened away, and tend to fly to the feeder once other birds have left, particularly the jays, who wear their bright blues like cops on the beat.

We have an abundance of woodpeckers, too. As mentioned in other stories, I have seen four kinds of them at our feeders, including the rarely-sighted pileated woodpeckers, which are big birds, larger even than the red-headed and red-bellied varieties. I have seen them below the house in the woods, but on a rare occasion I have seen them hit the feeder and dart off; I found a feather from one a few months ago.

Reading up on woodpeckers has taught me that there are actually eight types of them in Indiana, and my sighting of a yellow-bellied sapsucker wandering our back yard two months ago reinforced that not all birds visit our feeders. I have yet to get a photo, but it isn't that uncommon to see three varieties on the same tree at the same time. The downys, in their variegated coats, may be the most common.

Perhaps the most familiar birds we see are the juncos and chickadees and sparrows; each providing a splash of color to the otherwise dreary days. They and the nuthatches make quick raids of the feeders, mostly to snatch a seed and dash away to knock it back like a shot of whiskey.

We buy birdseed by the 50-pound bag; it gets expensive, particularly when we consider just how much of it is going to the squirrels or gets wasted on the wet ground. But we also consider it a good investment, one that pays dividends in color on these gray and melancholy days.

A Tough Month to Love

February 13, 2017

With apologies to my math teacher friends, I

have to admit that I agree with Skyler, the late Jeff MacNelly's little bird hero of the classic cartoon strip, *Shoe*.

Posed at his school desk in one cartoon, a bored look grimly spread across his face, Skyler claims that February is "the Algebra class of months." I, too, found the pace of my math courses nearly glacial, and as far as months go, well, February often has a similar feel to it.

Skyler also claimed that Chubby Checker wrote *Oliver Twist*, but that's beside the point. February, despite being the shortest month, takes a long time to go away. It may be designated as "Black History Month" and "American Heart Month" and "National Bird-Feeding Month" and "National Library Lovers Month," all noble observations, but getting to March involves a groundhog that repeatedly disappoints us, a sun that stubbornly stays in bed, and the occasional Canadian freight train cold front.

By the way, February is also "Return Shopping Carts to the Supermarket Month," and—I am not making this up—"Spunky Old Broads" month. I'm not sure who lobbied for that last one, but I imagine they were worth knowing and still play canasta.

Of course, February does have several redeeming qualities: Valentine's Day—which some curmudgeons feel is no more than a marketing ploy—and one of the most underappreciated federal holidays: President's Day. I like that holiday, and it has little to do with perhaps having a day off from school—if we don't have to use it to make up a snow day. I merely feel George Washington and Abraham Lincoln, despite having a day designated in their honor, are grossly overlooked, even in school lessons. Perhaps the current political climate will change our attitudes, but I doubt it.

Statistics do, indeed, back up my hypothesis about February being—as far as months go—a loser. Gallup Polls as far back as 1947 have asked Americans what months and days of the weeks they most favor, and since that time February has never gotten out of last place.

The most complete set of stats comes out of the 2005 poll, the last time the survey was conducted; in it, February and January sat dismally below March in the standings, both garnering just 2 percent of the votes—the Michael Dukakis of months, I suppose.

Clearly, the poll also determined that winter is our least-favorite season, although since '47 it has improved a bit, from a low of just 4 percent to 11 percent about 60 years later; online shopping must be responsible for that.

It came as no surprise to me that the age of the person polled had a lot to do with what month they most favored. It goes without saying that younger Americans enjoy the summer more than the other seasons—they are out of school—but even this old teacher has to admit that spring and fall are my favorite seasons, with a slight edge going to autumn. That first bracing breeze out of the north and the fall colors make

October my favorite month; it may sound bizarre, but I love to work in my yard when the leaves are beginning to drop; I like sweaters too.

Despite its terrible reputation, a lot of great things have happened in February. For instance, in 1876 the National League of baseball was founded—it later became the Major Leagues; the first automated envelope gumming machine was invented by John Sherman of Ames, Mass., in 1898; The Beatles went on the *Ed Sullivan Show* for the first time in 1964; and in 1928, Ed Shoemaker invented the La-Z-Boy recliner. February was also the month in 1958 when the U.S. Air Force managed to lose an atomic bomb off the coast of Savannah, Ga. Other than those things, no one else much noticed what went on in Februaries past because they were most likely sleeping or complaining about the crummy weather.

I discovered many more interesting facts while I watched it rain the other day. For instance, Monday isn't the least-favorite day of the week to Americans; it's Tuesday. Friday is number one, and most of us aren't even off from work that day; I imagine the anticipation of sleeping in on Saturday morning gives Friday a boost in the ratings, unless those optimists are like me and wake up at 3 a.m. anyway.

I really shouldn't badmouth February; it is often a beautiful month. Just last week, an early evening snow fell and covered our landscape in a light blanket of white. Cardinals and chickadees sat in our trees in between runs to the birdfeeders, not unlike ornaments that decorate a Christmas tree. And, regardless of the weather, I have a good job and a healthy family, and I am going to become a grandpa for a second time this summer—life is good, even when the month throws us those drab, sleety curveballs.

February is also "National Grapefruit Month" and "Potato Lovers Month" and "Chocolate Lovers Month," the latter a bit ironic since it is also "Dental Health Month."

Now that I think of it, maybe February does have a good side.

The Man and the Moon

February 27, 2017

I awoke early one morning a few weeks ago, a bright full moon slashing a band of light across my face through a partially-opened bedroom blind. As has become my habit over the passing years, I threw the covers aside and, by then, fully awake, padded about the house, looking through windows and re-checking locked doors.

I couldn't help but notice the strange glow of my yard, illuminated by a silent silver lamp, by then descending in the western sky. Everywhere I looked the trees cast lanky and strange shadows that I couldn't have possibly seen at any other time; it looked like a Rockwell Kent nightscape.

The moon has always fascinated me, and so, until I grew cold, I stood at a living room window a while, partially wondering if I'd be able to get back to sleep much before I had to ready myself for work a few hours later. Mostly I just gazed at our closest celestial neighbor; it is a most mysterious thing. In a general way, I can comprehend its phases and cycles, but I can't help but wonder, despite our country's flag being planted there long ago—forever stiff in some imaginary breeze—if the moon is keeping secrets from us.

In his wonderfully detailed little book, *Moon,* writer Bernd Brunner says that each generation has a "collective perception of what the moon is, means, and symbolizes." He adds, "In other words, there is not one moon, but many, each particular to a different culture. So to see the moon from the perspective of earlier peoples, we must try to shed all we have learned about it—at least for now."

Such is the case for me, and those of my generation. Born in the 1950's, my perceptions of the moon were first steeped in science fiction, in lavishly illustrated comic books and by poorly outfitted actors in low-budget movies; they often held ray guns and wore plastic bubbles over their heads.

The moon held—at least until the summer of 1969—an untouchable quality for those my age, even after John Kennedy pronounced what many felt was an unattainable goal. In May 1961, in a "special message to Congress," JFK said, "I believe that this nation should commit itself to achieving the goal, before this decade is out, of landing a man on the moon and returning him safely to the earth." Just a few months later—in fact, a day before my fifth birthday—he added, "We choose to go to the moon in this decade and do the other things, not because they are easy, but because they are hard."

By 1964, the year my mom bought my brother and me a telescope from the Sears and Roebuck Christmas "Wishbook," I couldn't imagine that one day soon men would be walking on the moon we eyed on starry nights. John and I used to set the telescope up in our back yard—more than once on the flat tarred roof of our back porch, until Mom found out—to look at the moon through a black cardboard tube until we had headaches.

I owned a "Golden Nature Guide" called *Stars* by then—it cost $1—and I spent a good bit of time in my top bunk bed, a metal reading lamp warming my scalp, and poured over the book's 150 illustrations. Some of the pictures were accurate depictions of what our super telescopes could see, but much of the work was pure fiction—what the surface of Mars looked like, for instance. Some of the "science" about the moon in those days wasn't much more than speculative; we had not left our footprints in its dust, hadn't scooped up its rocks, or driven on its surface in a modified dune buggy.

I know we have the web to surf these days, that virtually everything and anything can be found with the click of a finger. It is a great tool—one that I have used for this very piece—but in some ways I feel it has hurt our collective imaginations, our ingenuity, perhaps our inspiration. The subject of the moon may hold the best example of that. I am certainly glad I did not have a computer or the internet as a boy, for I am never bored as long as I have a book, and I never tire of looking at a night sky either, particularly now that I have a camera lens that gives me the moon much like that old telescope of ours.

Although I can pick out a few points of light in the night sky—Polaris and the "dippers" and Venus—astronomy, for the most part, confounds me. I know there are apps that will guide me as I gaze into the heavens, yet I rarely take the time to identify the constellations I am seeing; it is something I hope to amend in my retirement years, and, yes, I will use my computer to help me do it.

But the moon, I seem to understand a bit better, perhaps because it always shows us the same face. The huge crater, Tycho, some 100 million years old—quite young as far as astronomers are concerned—is always in the same place and the moon is virtually without seasons. It has a tilt of only about 1.5 degrees, and the gravity—or lack of it—there would have enabled me years ago to dunk a basketball on a goal nearly 59 feet high.

Unlike the ancients, I know the moon isn't smooth, nor is it made of cheese, as some believed in the 16th Century; that old telescope and common sense have taught me that much. But whether it be George Melies' turn-of-the-century film, *A Trip to the Moon* (famous for the "The Man in the Moon" getting a rocket ship in his eye) or Andy Williams singing "Moon River," whether I am "shooting for the moon" or hearing Ralph Kramden threatening to send Alice "straight to the moon," I moon over the moon, particularly when it is a full one. I guess that makes me a lunatic.

Hope Is the Thing with Feathers

March 13, 2017

The mild weather last month put just about everyone I know in a green grass mood before we ever turned the page on March.

My forsythia bushes were already blooming in late February, that is until a fast-moving cold front blasted through, but they'll come back soon. I have seen patches of daffodils smiling near the crooked cement of long-gone hillside house foundations too, and I expect to see redbuds earlier this year than ever before.

Although spring seems to be a two-steps forward, one-step back kind of thing for the first few weeks of March—with a bit of raw wind and snow thrown in—it appears to have a toehold now. Of course, one of its signs is the arrival of robins, those orange-breasted bug-eating machines with bad tempers.

I was already seeing them last month—even in January—and that may mean that a few of the hardiest of them rode out the winter here, shivering to stay warm and following vegan diets.

Robins have been held up as signs of spring for centuries, and rightly so. Although it is nearly certain—according to the Cornell Lab of Ornithology—that some robins don't really migrate at all, we tend to see them more in the spring because we're more likely to either be outdoors ourselves, or gazing through windows wishing we were.

My *Audubon Field Guide to North American Birds* merely states that robins can be found in Indiana in "all seasons," and surprisingly, 60 percent of their regular diet is berries. Their proverbial feasts on worms are solely on a "smoke 'em if you got 'em" basis, primarily in the spring and summer.

Indiana State University professor emeritus Peter Scott, who specializes in plant-pollinator interactions and ornithology, thinks that seeing large numbers of robins is a "true sign of spring."

"I have about a 100 today in the fields around my place, on a slightly frosty morning," Scott told me a dozen days ago. "They are presumably getting worms and similar things—definitely feeding—although they have no song. From my casual observation, there is a period of a couple of weeks when the fields are full of robins, and then much less so. It is hard to tell with these birds what percentage is migrating further north, or arriving to breed around here; a mix, no doubt."

Scott also told me that robins seem to be more common in southern and central Indiana during the winter, and are most often found during the winter in bigger cities where there are more fruit-bearing ornamentals trees and shrubs.

"Robins need invertebrates (worms, beetles, and moths) and/or fruit. In freezes, there is little suitable animal food, and the natural fruit supply dwindles in winter, so hence the need for migration, formerly more than now," Scott added. He also told me that robins don't feed on seeds, and rarely, if ever, on suet, so don't expect them at your feeders.

I have noticed more robins along my wood line for weeks now. They are notoriously grumpy after they have nested and are raising young; expect hatchlings to be begging for meals by early April. A baby out of its spring nest—or the presence of a housecat nearby—can set robins into Hitchcockian frenzies, but for now, anyway, they hop about jabbing their beaks into my lawn in search of night crawlers, and do so rather meekly.

Like most birds, there is a reasonably clear distinction between the males and females. "You can tell males from females," Scott tells me. The males are blacker on the head, and generally brighter overall than the browner and grayer, drabber females. Both have the rufous [rust-colored] breast, but again it's brighter in the male."

Their habit of feeding on the ground makes robins obvious targets for snakes and hawks and a host of other predators, but its color is the topic of Native American folklore.

According to one legend, the robin supposedly got its red-orange breast by approaching a dying fire, then fanning it to save a freezing man and boy from the cold. There is a similar tale surrounding the origin of the European robin, which I might add doesn't look that much like its American cousin. Actually, robins found across the Atlantic are considered flycatchers, while American robins are thrashers.

Robins also find their place in literature, something of which I am more familiar. I can't remember seeing a single robin on the grounds around the poet's old manse when my wife and I visited Amherst years ago, but the reclusive Emily Dickinson must have, for she mentions robins in about a dozen of her poems.

Dickinson did not give her poetry titles, so other than assigning numbers to them, editors normally just used each poem's first line to identify it. In "I dreaded that first robin, so," the poet actually dislikes the approaching spring, for its bright colors and bird songs and bees only remind her of the dreary depression that she can't overcome. At one point in the poem, Dickinson even refers to herself as the "Queen of Calvary," a woman who is suffering beyond description.

However, in other poems, she calls the robin, "a Gabriel," as being "cherubic," and as something that will be missed when the summer is gone. In another, one of her best, Dickinson writes of the birds in her trees as symbols of optimism and promise.

"Hope is the thing with feathers/That perches in the soul," she says. Of course, robins remind us that she is right.

The Beautiful Cartography of Our Minds
March 27, 2017

It will probably come as no surprise to anyone who knows me that I still use a road atlas. Despite having GPS capabilities on both my phone and in my car, I prefer to read and use a road map. It is a habit I got into when, as a boy, all I could do was dream of going someplace, and I have no intention of kicking the habit anytime soon.

Maps are part of my learning DNA. Those of my generation spent a lot of time studying and making them in school—coloring them, tracing them as homework, memorizing them for tests, and I am forever grateful. The spatial thinking skills of map-making were enhanced with salt and cake coloring and toothpicks, for nearly every student of my era was required to make at least one salt map, probably at about the same time we were constructing baking soda volcanoes and adding to our leaf collections.

As we better prepare the current generation of schoolchildren for taking standardized tests, we are, unfortunately, losing precious time for maps, and, yes, I do blame those handy little apps and cell phones and curriculum-building buttinskis. As long as their batteries are charged, the world is apparently at our children's fingertips. But "left" on a "Google Map" doesn't really teach them much about directions, and not knowing how to read a real map won't help them find a store in the mall either. There are still practical reasons we all need to sharpen our map skills, and I won't leave us 60-somethings out of that equation either; we all need the skills of mental map-making.

I was encouraged when I read the recent social media post of a friend who watched the local "Geography Bowl" competition a few weeks ago; he said he was embarrassed that the grade-schoolers he saw knew so much more about the subject than he did. However, an alarming string of studies shows those children as being atypical. American kids, and their parents, aren't very map literate.

I do realize that science and technology have left salt maps and baking soda volcanoes behind, but not the educational principles behind them. In a report that appeared in *U.S. News and World Report* in October 2015, education reporter Lauren Camera says: "A new report from the Government Accountability Office found that more than half of Social Studies teachers spend 10 percent or less of their time on geography. Social Studies is the umbrella subject under which geography is taught, along with things like history, civics, and economics. What's more, a majority of states do not require geography courses in middle school or high school. As of 2013, only 17 states required a geography course in middle school and 10 states required a geography course for students to graduate from high school."

I wouldn't imagine that things have improved much in the last four years, but it's not schools that are solely responsible for teaching map skills. Many of the first and best books I can recall reading had maps in them, and I still like books that include them, particularly historical novels that put me in places I have never been, nor can go. To me, great writers enable readers to walk on real ground, and those—both young and old—who can create a cartography of the mind, right down to the streets and sidewalks that live on the pages, have been handed a great gift. Robert Louis Stevenson knew that in *Treasure Island,* and Jerry West, who penned *The Happy Hollisters* series did too; and often those books included maps, sometimes secret and hand-drawn …

Of course, my map-reading partner is my wife, who reminded me that had it not been for a map, we wouldn't have had many of our travel adventures together. Setting one's course via GPS can help us get from Point A to Point B more quickly, but we mostly travel by instinct rather than schedule.

An example comes from a trip to the Big Horn Mountains of Wyoming a few years ago. While on a stop in eastern Iowa—at the Herbert Hoover Presidential Library—Joanie picked up a historic map of Iowa at the visitor's center. "Look," she said, holding the accordion-like folds of the glossy paper back for me to see. "John Wayne's birthplace is highlighted here," she said as she pointed to Madison County, considerably off the beaten path for us as we headed for Nebraska.

Our unintended trip to Winterset was a treasure; it could have very well been marked with a big red X. Not only did we learn most of what we wanted to about Wayne, right down to his original *True Grit* eye patch, but we found our way to most of the county's well-known covered bridges, made famous by both writer James Waller and director/actor Clint Eastwood.

In recent years, as I revert to childhood once more in what I hope is a clear-headed, yet nostalgic way, I have taken to collecting local and state maps. Although I feel it important that I know where Sudan and Yemen, Pyongyang and Jakarta are, I also think it good to know the topography of my own landscape, of my county and hometown, of the geology and geography of the place. Yellowing atlases and plat maps show me the canal beds and railroad lines and ghost towns where now only wild grape vines and honeysuckle and slag heaps remain.

When cruising the oft-traveled roads of memory, I still see myself riding with my grandfather in his blue Chevy pickup truck, he with one hand on the wheel, and me across the seat with a road map spread out in my lap. As we ambled through the hills of Kentucky and Tennessee on curving Highway 421, I served as 12-year-old navigator and co-pilot, figuring critical gas mileage and estimating the towns we had yet to go through before we could fire up our two-burner gas stove for supper. We bunked pretty much anyplace we felt we'd be left alone.

"That was Burning Springs," I'd tell him. "The next town is Fall Rock." All that time, the map gave us both a sense of adventure, for no digital thing could tell us in those days what was around the next corner or over the next mountain.

We had to find that out for ourselves.

A Beach Is Good for the Soul

July 17, 2017

I have written many times over the years about our annual pilgrimage to the Lake Michigan shoreline, yet, here I am again, trying to relate to my friends just how much the blue-green water and its waves mean to us.

This year, we headed a little farther north to a rented house in South Haven, for the wonderful Great Depression-era cabins that we have stayed in for years also require rigorous trips up and down a steep set of stairs to and from the beach. Despite being senior citizens now, Joanie and I can still hack the climb, but we thought it best not to put our pregnant daughter-in-law through such daily workouts, lest we have our second grandchild earlier than expected.

In a series of features about yet a more extensive tour of Michigan last summer—we left the rest of the family at home for that one—I extolled the virtues of the many towns we visited, but had little to say about South Haven, which boasts a wonderful downtown, tastefully-designed homes, and a splendid old red lighthouse. It is a beautiful little town, but after the day we spent there we came away feeling rushed, as if we had been through a typical tourist trap wringer and left hanging out to dry. I take all of that back now, for we loved the place this summer, and I have learned, once again, that first impressions are often wrong.

Despite a few early days of very cool weather that kept everyone out of the water, and a stiff breeze that tossed our hair about like salads, we enjoyed good food, a nice daily walk or bike ride to the beach, and a quiet little sandy promontory above the water where we could hide in the tall grass, pretty much away from everyone else.

My grandson and son eventually made it into the chilly lake, but not without a little teeth chattering and shivering. I, on the other hand, did as I always do: watched the water and read books and dozed in a beach chair, and then I did it all over again. That is my idea of a real vacation, with a few crosswords thrown in for good measure.

Red warning flags blew stiffly in a rather raw wind as we first arrived at South Haven. Typical road construction along I-94, that seems to be in place like a plague of locusts in time for our annual trip, had slowed us in getting there. So after unpacking, the late hour left us little time to do much more than eat supper, bundle up a bit, and head to the lake to watch the sun set. We are rarely disappointed in a Lake Michigan sunset, and despite hugging ourselves to stay warm, we witnessed a blue-ribbon winner that first night.

Joanie and I spent most of the rest of our days on the beach, her hair uncharacteristically stuffed under one of my ball caps, and both of us toting books under one arm and chairs under the other. We soon discovered that several bikes—we chose retro-Schwinns—were available for our use, and I eventually became a pro at strapping everything we needed to the back of mine. It did take a few minutes to adjust to the bike's coaster brake, for I don't think I've used one since I was 12.

Over the course of the week I filled the spaces around my crosswords with lists of observations that really described—in scribbles—our stay at South Haven. For instance, we noticed that there were virtually no stones on these beaches, so our traditional rock-skipping competition had to be called off. We also noticed a number of ducks flying overhead; we never see those where we normally stay, and one eventually posed rather nicely for my camera one morning. Within an hour of snapping the mallard's picture, I took another of a "Jolly Roger" flying over a pleasure boat quite far out on the lake, but we never felt a pillaging raid was imminent.

As usual, I noted how the different angle of the sun—from the morning through the supper hours—changed the color of the lake all day. In fact, color is what I most notice on these trips. Milkweed was growing everywhere along the beach, and I saw monarch butterflies flitting about it, and black squirrels in the yards, and brown house wrens everywhere.

Of course, the gulls (both ring-billed and herring) are always present along the beach. Most are looking for handouts of cookies and crackers, but they dominated the view nearly as much as the incoming surf, often flying startling close to us. The birds I was most interested in, however, were the bank swallows that occupied the steep sandy cliff that we sat atop. I often walked down to the beach to try to catch them in a photo as they entered and exited the caverns they'd excavated in the banks, but was never able to do it. They were so fast, so nearly manic, that I could never get them in my viewfinder, so I eventually quit trying.

By our second or third day, the red flags had been replaced with yellow, and the temperatures lifted well into the 70's. Joanie and I biked down to the pier to walk out to the lighthouse—built in 1903 of cast iron and painted bright red—and to watch a few fisherman casting for steelhead. The beach near there was quite crowded, so we soon retreated and headed back to base for lunch.

It may sound odd, but my favorite day on the lake was one which promised rain. On one late afternoon, we could see storm clouds gathering to the west—even saw a waterspout off in the distance—and the sun played a game of tag with the lake, turning it alternating shades of blue, then green and brown as the waves stirred up sand along the beach. The marram grass bent in the strong breeze, and slowly, but surely, the beaches emptied as people grew tired of chasing umbrellas and hats, and the supper hour approached.

I stayed on to watch the show, and was glad I did. The choppy whitecaps and green water and purple-blue rain clouds came in across the distant pier, and just then I knew that I hadn't seen many places in my life that were much prettier.

On the mantle of the house we had rented, the owner had placed one of those typical beach-related curios, sometimes picked up at yard sales when the original buyer has grown tired of northern climes and has headed to Arizona. It was, if I recall now, a bit of driftwood glued to a small sign that read, "A beach is good for the soul."

It sure is.

CHAPTER TWO: Other Stories

The Cost of Convenience

August 8, 2015

As I drove past the bank on Central Street in Rosedale recently, I realized that the next time I walk through its doors may be the last time I step into the place.

The bank is closing next month, and it's yet another punch to the gut to an already dwindling little town that has seen its restaurant and hardware store, its ice cream shop and grocery store pull out or shut down in recent years.

I'm not in a snit and stuffing my mattress with cash, nor am I bunkering down in preparation of an impending economic apocalypse, but I'm not happy. I don't think the bank was losing money; I simply think it wasn't making enough of it. It was, in all probability, a victim of the convenience we now "enjoy."

We have been reminded that there are other banks in other towns fairly close by; disgruntled as we may be, we can use those. We can procure loans and deposit savings online. We can grab cash at an ATM when we're at dozens of other "convenient" locations too. We have also been told that we can call, email, and text our way to good service. I guess it's a wonder the shutdown hasn't happened sooner.

This isn't a rant against the bank's board or president; business is business, and apparently our locality wasn't doing enough of it. It has, in many ways, ended up in the dust, just like the Rosedale National Bank that once sat on Main Street. It, by the way, boasted 4-percent interest rates on savings deposits in 1922, and claimed to be the "bank of friendly service." It died during the Great Depression.

I do worry, though, that the progress we see in convenience ends up biting us in the end, a phrase I use as both pun and for argument's sake.

Many of the residents of our town—and I don't just mean those who never quite figured out how to program their VCRs—actually enjoyed walking into the bank (and our defunct lumber yard and dime store and pharmacy, which have been gone for years and years) and being greeted by a face and a voice, rather than the glow of an electronic screen.

Several others who deposit money from their places of business—our gas station and beauty parlor, our variety store and the many local farms, among others—found the bank an important extension of their lives, not just a place to gab or get out of the sun or grab a free calendar.

Although my wife most often does our banking, I was a regular customer, too. I rarely ever found the bank empty, and often saw it congested, a line of idling cars pulling past the drive-through window, and folks standing two or three deep at the walk-up counter.

I found it nice that the tellers there—one of whom I taught in school and another who used to share her favorite recipes with customers—greeted me by name. Because they knew me, I believe they took special care to do their work carefully. It's good to know that they'll not be losing their jobs, although they may have to drive a bit farther now to get to them.

Is convenience hurting our communities? I think it is, at least incrementally, although we have been seeing those black clouds on the horizon and hearing the doomsdayers long before online banking and email, self-serve gas stations and drive-up mortuaries came along. In time, however, I am afraid that the last generation that did business with a handshake and in person will be gone, and our culture will be the less for it.

Tom Steiger is a professor of Sociology at Indiana State University and the director of the Center for Student Research and Creativity. He told me—ironically via email from Oregon a few days ago—that because "face-to-face communication is hard," we'll continue to find ways to avoid interacting, unless it is something we want to do.

"Are we losing something? Yes. Is it the end of civilization? About as much so as what the telephone and cheap long distance did to the art of letter writing. Ever read letters from relatives far away from before the '60s? I have all the letters my dad wrote home from the Philippines during World War II, and he wasn't a particularly gifted man. But those letters beat anything my kids could write today because they would call and tell me about it, or Skype it, or, heaven forbid, 'tweet' it," he said.

He added, "I think what you are seeing today is the result of more historical trends and social and economic forces than just the technology. The tech is just hastening that cultural change. Cultures change. But the pace of ours wears out many of us to be sure. I sometimes feel like I'm just holding on by a hangnail..."

Tom went on to say that as he wrote his reply to me, he was sitting in a busy coffee shop, and virtually everyone there was alone. The one couple who sat at a nearby table was not communicating; the man was reading a newspaper (yes, an actual paper copy), and the woman was on her phone. Everyone else was on a computer, except one girl who was writing on a yellow legal pad as she sipped her joe.

"Why are these people here?" Tom asked himself. "I could have had coffee in my [hotel] room and used the free wifi. But I wanted company, even if I haven't spoken to anyone. And so do these other folks... Despite all this alienating technology, people still gather."

Although I hope that another bank will come to our town to replace the one that is leaving, it is a dim hope at best. But I'm not sure it is just our safe deposit boxes and checking accounts that make us want to keep the bank; I think that many of us sense that we are losing yet another place, as Tom has said, to "gather." We have lost the coffee shop at the grocery store, the barber shop conversations, the house calls from the doctor in town, too.

I guess we had better get used to change.

A Hard Lesson with Yellow Jackets

August 31, 2015

Over the past 30 years or so, I have visited Dr. Thomas Nicholas' office for a number of reasons. Besides my yearly physical and blood work, I've most often found myself sitting in his High Street waiting room and nursing miserable sinuses that seek retribution from me for some unknown offense.

But most of my other trips to see Doc, or his partner, Daniel Dwyer, can be found in my bulging medical file under a notation that probably reads: "Dumb Things This Guy Has Done to Himself."

At one time or another, Dr. Tom has stitched, wrapped, iced, and injected my back, knees, elbows, shoulders, and neck. He's sewn gashes and taken out splinters too deep for a sewing needle to reach; he's torqued knees and thumped chests and probed my ears, nose, and eyes.

To put it mildly, he knows my innards better than I do, myself, so much better, in fact, that he no longer really has to go searching through that thick manila folder to tell me when I was last in with some similar malady; you see, I rarely learn from past mistakes.

A great example of that came a few weeks ago when I had to see Doc about a rash I'd developed after being stung—yet again—by a ground hornet. Now, before you think that I'm some pantywaist who runs to the doctor every time I have a boo-boo, I'll just say that after being stung while mowing grass one hot Saturday afternoon, I followed post-sting protocol rather well: I walked back to the house, popped a few antihistamine capsules, then slathered a little baking soda on my ankle, which is one of the vulnerable spots most often attacked when mowers are pushed, pulled, or ridden over hornets' well-camouflaged hideouts. I still had some mowing left to do, so after medicating, I headed back outdoors.

"You know," Doc said, after hearing my story, "I normally tend to find you to be a pretty smart man, but I'm not so sure your going back out to mow in the heat and humidity after being stung qualifies you for being very smart."

That's what I like about Doc: he's always very kind, very diplomatic when he thinks I've been an idiot. He told me that with my history of hornet stings, I really should have rested a while, got a cold compress on my ankle, and let Joanie keep an eye on me for a half-hour or so.

That "history" includes being stung a dozen or so times by yellow jackets over the years, and I have progressed from merely shaking off a painful little lump to now swelling up like Jabba the Hutt. I am apparently entering into a new phase of overreaction to stings, now developing rashes that make me look like an extra from the leper scene in *Papillon*. Next time, Doc says, I may not be so lucky; I believe he mentioned "compromised breathing and throat swelling…"

I had to admit to Doc that I did remember more than one instance when I've had to call him in after office hours to get an injection after being stung. A few years back, I was nailed several times on the hand and arm as I mowed a hillside dotted with old mole runs (a common home for hornet nests). Within 30 minutes I looked like a lobster in a pair of cargo shorts, so Joanie loaded me up for a trip to see Doc, who, I am sure, would have liked to have been somewhere else, yet he dutifully met me at the office.

Nicholas went on to explain that my rash might actually get a little worse before it got better. Since he loves to draw graphic examples for his patients on the backside of his prescription pads, he did so while telling me how my body was overreacting to the hornet's venom. I scratched and squirmed a bit and tried to look as though I understood his chemistry lesson, but I perked up when he directed his nurse to give me an injection. (They always say it will be in the "hip," but we know better, don't we?) I then watched as he scribbled in my file that this particular visit was for—I think I got it right—a "systematic allergic reaction to hymenoptera sting." I believe that's what I read, but Doc's kind of secretive with that file.

It is somewhat ironic that just a few columns

ago, I mentioned our nasty ground hornets and dry Indiana weather with August yet to come, but since then—particularly because one of them tried to kill me—I've done a little more reading about "hymenoptera." I've learned that what we often call a ground hornet or yellow jacket is actually a wasp of sorts, and that about a half-million people a year visit hospital emergency rooms because of insect stings and bites. I imagine that most of those instances happen when some poor unsuspecting slob like me runs his mower or tiller or weed trimmer over a spot in which yellow jackets have chosen to take up residence. And, as I have found out, they don't like the peace and quiet of their neighborhoods disturbed.

I've also discovered, quite by accident a few years ago when digging a drainage ditch, that yellow jackets build paper (they chew wood fibers into paper-like pulp) nests underground (not unlike the nests we see hanging from trees). They don't return to the same nests each year, since winter weather destroys them. A good hard freeze pretty well kills yellow jackets, although some that stay underground a while longer may survive a few weeks more. It is only the fertilized queens who will hang on to re-start the colony again the following spring.

Despite looking for it a good while, I never found the hidey-hole from which my assassin yellow jacket emerged, which means I am mowing with great care these days. If I do discover it, I'll not call in a napalm strike or seek my own personal revenge;

hornets are not my white whale. Whether I like it or not, they are actually pretty useful. My reading also tells me that they kill and eat all sorts of "nuisance" insects that hurt our crops and gardens; they love to gorge their young on housefly larvae, too.

And they have gone to great lengths over the years to keep my doctor in profitable business.

Grandparents Day Everyday from Now On

September 14, 2015

Being a teacher, I have gotten used to being called a rich variety of names, but despite another birthday that will have come and gone on the day before this story is to run, "Grandpa" has yet to be one of them.

That is about to change, and how appropriate that I celebrated this most recent of birthdays by knowing it was, in a way, the first Grandparents Day Joanie and I can unofficially call our own, too.

We are to be grandparents in just weeks, that is if my son and his wife, Lucy—and their obstetrician—are doing their math correctly. The grandbaby, our first, will arrive as a bit of a surprise, for no one, including the proud parents, knows whether it is to be a he or a she.

Regardless of gender, the scheduled appearance is to come in early October, and despite a long-standing policy on my behalf to never wish my life to pass too quickly, I have now suspended that conviction, for a few weeks anyway.

Grandparents Day became a national celebration too late for all but one of my grandparents to enjoy, and in the case of my Grandpa Roy, who outlived all the others by most of a decade, it came just a few months before he died.

But now, the first Sunday after Labor Day has blossomed into a full-blown holiday, with its own official flower—forget-me-nots—an entire week of celebratory school breakfasts with elementary-aged grandchildren, its own section in the greeting card aisles, and a permanent place on the calendar. I heartily approve.

Our preparation for the big day has not come without some expense. I spent much of the summer with my buddy, Joe, remodeling a bedroom that is to be the baby's nursery away from home, and my wife and I had to practically get bank financing for the stroller we bought for the kids; we even saw models that had USB ports and DVD players, even GPS systems. I think "rich Corinthian leather" was offered, too.

Just today, I reminded Joanie that we had better get our old crib set up, that is if we can find it in our overstuffed attic. Many of our children's toys have been bagged and stowed away for years now, but we haven't a rattle, changing table, or Playskool mobile to our names.

We are far behind the "new arrival" re-learning curve, it seems, and I just remembered that I have yet to refinish an old toy chest I bought years ago at an auction, although I suppose I have some time yet before it will be needed.

Before I know it, I'll be childproofing the house, capping electrical outlets, moving household cleaners to upper shelves, and dusting off baby gates and swing sets. But we have no intention of resurrecting diaper pails and pelican bibs any time soon.

We have gotten much advice from friends and family members with grandparental experience under their belts. We know we are a little late in getting into the grandma and grandpa business for the first time, but I think we will get in the groove with relative ease. Both of us loved our grandparents dearly, and I imagine we have learned our lessons well from them.

We are determined to ignore the "spoil-them-rotten-then-send-them-home" mantra; we didn't allow our kids to use the sofa as a trampoline or re-do the walls in crayon, so I doubt whether our grandchildren will get away with that either, although I will have a liberal ice cream-eating policy, I'm sure.

I won't try to speak for my wife, but it always seemed as though my grandparents, particularly my dad's parents, had time for me. My Grandma Blanche was only 60 when she passed, but she loaded the few precious years we had together with fun and adventures and lessons and affection. Because we lived next door to them, my paternal grandparents became our surrogate parents and friends and teachers; they hauled us to church, shoveled food into us as if we were racehorses, spanked our bottoms, and hugged us a lot.

I can speak for Joanie when I say that we plan to love our grandkids, too, and I hope we love them enough to invest the rest of our lives into theirs. I hope we'll be able to tell them no, right along with yes, to be silly with them, to listen to them, to help them grow, to be the best teachers they ever had.

We want to put great books into their hands, help them be interested in things, hope they'll come to love the natural world outside their doors, walk with them, talk with them, haul them to wherever they need to go.

A few summer weeks ago, I sat talking in a local café with my friend, Bill Wolfe, who I imagine is as good a grandpa as he is a sculptor and painter. Upon hearing that I was soon to be a grandpa, he said, "You know, Mike, if you think you love your kids, it'll be hard to believe that you can love your grandkids even more."

We do love our children, and it's hard to imagine loving anyone more. It sure will be fun trying, though.

The Last Guy in Town to Let You Down

October 12, 2015

My brother let me know last week that Russell Shadley had died. Russell lived in Chicago, and like his mom and dad and sister before him, he valiantly fought a battle with cancer, but eventually lost the war. He was 64.

My life, and the lives of those I grew up with, is linked to those of Russell's family, in that my parents and his parents were the best of friends. My dad and Clarence Russell Shadley—better known as "Shag"—graduated together from Otter Creek High School in the Class of 1948.

The "Class Personalities" section of their senior yearbook named Shag the class "Hair Comber;" my dad, its "Biggest Bluffer" and the "Wittiest." In one photo, they stand a few feet apart in the back row of the bleachers, both in white T-shirts, my dad impossibly skinny, and Shag, wearing suspenders, boasting wavy hair and impish eyes. They looked ready to conquer the world.

A few pages later, the class census (all kinds of wonderful things like it seem to be lost on modern annuals now) mentioned that my dad was "from the County Line, never stays out late, and wants to be a model husband."

He most definitely did live a few feet from Parke County, but was undoubtedly speaking with tongue firmly in cheek about the other two qualities. Shag, the census read, "is a character, likes women, never works, and wants to be a magician."

Most of the members of that class never really lost contact with one another. Each year, as far back as I can remember, my mom and dad packed a cooler with ice and Dr. Pepper, filled a picnic basket with fried chicken and macaroni salad, and headed to Deming Park for a summer Sunday afternoon of reliving the past with the Shadleys and the families of the other 40-odd Otter Creek grads.

It was a wonderful day that made wonderful memories for us, and while our parents reminisced and laughed, the children played together and explored the park. The blueberry sno-cones, the one-eyed alligator, and the miniature train rides are among the best memories I have of those days, but "Shag the Magician" and his wonderful family gave me even more.

A few times a year, Mom, Dad, my sister and brother and I all would pile into our old car and drive across pothole-riddled Flat Iron Road to Danville, Ill., to spend time with the Shadleys. Shag, who had, indeed, become a magician (a very good one who had performed in younger days with Blackstone), still had to work a day job at a sporting goods store to feed his brood.

In their huge, old two-story house that had no front yard and sat on a busy street (Shag often had to beat on its clunky radiators with his shoe), we'd spend a day and early evening, a simmering supper already on the stove.

Shag's wife, Ann, was a remarkably warm and funny lady, and their six kids—Russell, Jeff, Chris, Angela, Teresa and Annette—all seemed to be interesting mixes of both parents. It didn't take five minutes to see that although Shag was the life of the party in that house, Ann was the heart of it; her messy kitchen, resplendent with crusty pots and greasy pans, produced magnificent and prodigious meals, and although she allowed her kids to literally trash a big utility room with their countless toys and shoes, the rest of her house was both spotless and off limits to everyone but guests. I remember her always having a smile on her face and a spoon in her hand. Everyone loved her.

Time at the Shadleys was magical for us. We were country kids, but their children had, for the most part, spent their lives in the city, immune to traffic noise and close neighbors and the blares of sirens. They had a worldliness about them that gave us a new way of looking at things, and I still recall the evening after supper when we younger boys explored the neighborhood and ended up in a scrape with a few kids several streets away. The gang chased us all the way back home, but not before we had pelted them with rotten fall tomatoes that we had picked up as we ran through an alley garden.

Certain that we were safe upstairs, I taunted one of the toughs by standing in front of a screened window with my tongue out. He promptly hit me in the face with a perfectly thrown tomato that he'd grabbed during the pursuit, and although its stench made me gag, I had to laugh—still do.

Russell and my brother would almost immediately disappear after we arrived in Danville—being five years older than the rest of us gave them unrestrained freedom—and it was their adventures together that fueled our memories of that wonderful family and those days.

One of the first places that John and Russell would often end up was a local discount store in Danville that "specialized" in selling seconds and discontinued items. John claimed that the store boasted a huge outdoor sign with hundreds of light bulbs, of which, "maybe, 32 worked."

The pair would walk the aisles for hours and pick through displays of flawed and often bizarre merchandise until their laughter drew the attention of the store's management; more than once, they were asked to leave. Whether it be the mislabeled "Boly Hibles" or the "slightly irregular" brassieres (both B and D cups)—that required coupons for purchase—John and Russell would literally laugh until they were sick or thrown out, whichever came first.

Ann's mother, Grandma Hanrahan, often came to the Shadleys' place. A devout Catholic, she once inspected the rebellious Russell's bedroom and discovered a poster of the Cuban revolutionary, Che Guevara, that had been pinned to the wall. She proclaimed how happy she was that Russell had "found Jesus," but I don't think Shag and Ann had it in them to let her down. And so it went.

Before we'd leave the house on those memorable nights, Shag would inevitably (we begged him) grab a hat and don a wand and put on a little magic show in the living room for us. With his pencil thin cigarillos always smoldering, and his pinky ring flashing, he'd entertain us for most of an hour with effortless sleight-of-hand. I know I fell asleep on the way home still awed by it, by him.

Ann was only 42 when she passed in 1972, and Shag took on a job as a maintenance man at Resurrection Cemetery in Danville, where she was buried; he continued, as well, to pick up shows at local clubs and schools, when he could.

The cemetery job was, I think, the best way Shag had of staying closer to the heart of that once-magical house of his, but he just told my dad with a smile that he was simply "the last guy in town to let you down."

The Curious Case of the Oxford Comma

October 26, 2015

Knowing that I am a bit of a punctuation grump, my daughter recently sent a poster to me that read: "You can have my Oxford comma when you pry it from my cold, dead, and lifeless hands." Since I am a fan of that oft-argued bit of ink, I plan to post the sign in my classroom.

No matter how many times I use an Oxford comma in my stories, my Tribune-Star editor, Susan Duncan, an otherwise sensible and agreeable lady, unceremoniously hacks it out. Often called the serial comma, an Oxford comma—named for its mandatory use by Oxford University Press for years—is, according to the Oxford Dictionary, itself, "an optional comma before the word 'and' at the end of a list."

For me, there is no option; I am driven to use the Oxford, compelled by my grade school upbringing under stern grammatical taskmasters and my own obsessive-compulsive love for clarification; I even married an Oxford comma devotee, who inserts them into my copy when I have committed the occasional sin of omission. I'm pretty certain that our marriage vows included a serial comma or two.

Despite critics, including the usually cranky H.L. Mencken, who labeled the Oxford both "prissy" and "un-American," I am a devotee. I was raised as a writer in the belief that if my writing was not understood by a reader, I was mostly to blame. There's something Freudian about that, I suppose.

I am also convinced—despite it being highly improbable—that at least one of my old high school English teachers (still amazed, perhaps, that my name and the word "writer" are used in the same sentence) is, at this very moment, poring over today's story, his or her pen dripping red ink.

To be fair to Susan, I have to say that she knows the "Associated Press Stylebook" like her grandma's favorite recipes, and it demands that the Oxford be exorcised. Newspaper stories are formatted using the concise and persnickety space-saving AP style, so her handbook does not equivocate with the serial comma. It simply states: "Do not use commas before a conjunction in a simple series." How can anyone argue with that?

I can. I don't have much journalism in my background—which keeps Susan quite busy—so I continue to stick with tradition, subversively slipping the old Oxford in whenever I can, hopeful that she'll miss it just once. I also confess that as my columns go into book form, I retrace Susan's steps and place every one of those commas back into my text, snickering, but acknowledging that no one probably even notices.

Are newspapers going to argue that there is dramatic cost savings in ink expenditures due to Oxford comma deletion practices? I'm sure that statistics do exist for such a thing, but even though many editors want to wipe out the Oxford for good, I secretly believe that more and more of them, in quietly rebellious moments, recall their early grammar days and the venerable *Strunk and White's The Elements of Style*, that simply states: "In a series of three or more terms with a single conjunction, use a comma after each term except the last."

For those of you who have managed to stay with me this far in a column about grammar—the school day equivalent of working the rock pile—I have to mention that the Oxford comma remains a much-debated and controversial subject, particularly of late with those who've attempted to inject some grammatical sense into their social media entries. Yes, there are those among us who actually edit texts and "tweets," even correct poor grammar on their Facebook pages.

Read the following:

"I love the old red, white and blue."

"I love the old red, white, and blue."

Now, I imagine that most readers can't see much of a difference there, and they might appreciate what many grammarians say about the Oxford: that there has been much ado made about nothing.

But what about in this case:
"Doreen looked forward to the romantic date with her husband, a bricklayer and an amateur photographer."
"Doreen looked forward to the romantic date with her husband, a bricklayer, and an amateur photographer."

I have to think that the serial comma in this instance makes a big difference, particularly to the future of Doreen's marriage. Of course, we could simply re-write the passage, but that ruins my argument.

So I have come to the conclusion that when it comes to the Oxford, there are few absolutes, that it is needed on many occasions, but it's not on others. As Joe Bunting, a contributor to *thewritepractice.com*, tells me, "It's not essential but in certain situations it is helpful." I had to admit to Joe that I'd have placed a comma between essential and the conjunction in his response, but that's just me.

Mary Norris, who wrote a wonderful piece about grammar—including using the Oxford—for *The New Yorker* a while back, mentioned something that E.B. White, of the aforementioned *Strunk and White's*, wrote years ago. White said that before he began working on the famous style guide, he was the kind of writer who did not have "any exact notion of what is taking place under the hood."

I, too, find myself driving the car of grammar and mechanics without knowing much about all of its various engine parts. For instance, I try to prevent my students from beginning sentences with conjunctions, yet I often give in to that temptation as I write my stories for this newspaper.

After all, the AP Stylebook has no rule against it. And Susan says I can.

The Country Boy Who Went to Korea

November 11, 2015

It is in the inevitable process of cleaning up and clearing out the things our parents leave behind when they pass that we learn more about them, perhaps even see them in ways we never could when they lived and breathed. Such was the case after my parents died, and has been for my wife and her sisters in the seven years since their dad, Gilbert Dickey, left us.

A few weeks ago, as the sisters cleaned up some things for their mother, Joanie came across her dad's letters from his Army days in Korea. They were written to his older sister, Martha Jean McCarthy, who had not been married long by then, nearly 65 years ago. Not having the time to sit down right away to read them, Joanie handed the large envelope filled with the letters to me, saying, "I thought you'd like to read these."

So on a Sunday morning, sloppy and unshaven and still in the grips of a bout with the flu, I sat down with a cup of coffee to read a letter or two.

Instead, I read them all—more than two dozen of them—and along the way came to know my father-in-law a little better, and miss him a little more.

Gib was 23 when he left home for Korea. He had

never traveled far from his father's Parke County farm, outside of the time he spent disliking a short stay studying engineering at Purdue. He wanted more than anything else to farm, so by the time the United States was fighting in Korea, he had a girlfriend he planned to marry and a dream to someday own his own ground.

But the war got in the way of those plans; he was drafted in 1950, shipped out for his first training to Fort Campbell, Kentucky, and within a few months was on a ship headed to Japan. He told my son, who interviewed him for a grade school Veterans Day project years ago, that he was the only man in his unit who didn't seem to be affected by the motion sickness brought on by the voyage, but the stench of vomit was so overwhelming in his quarters that he soon was just as sick as everyone else.

It didn't take long for Gib to head to the front, or be close to it. But instead of complaining much about the occasional shelling from the North Koreans, his biggest gripes seemed to be about the cold Korean wind and his superior officers, one sergeant, in particular, who harassed him about having a dirty weapon.

An independent sort who always liked to make his own rules, Gib probably had problems taking any orders that had been given just to be given. By the way, his suspicions that the sergeant simply wanted someone to pick at were confirmed when he handed a friend's rifle in for inspection. His comrade's gun was usually held up as a sterling example of maintenance, but when Gib handed it over, he was reprimanded once again. But, because he could fix just about anything, he eventually won his critic over by keeping the latter's radio mended, and his rifle was no longer an issue.

Gib told me that his time in Korea was the loneliest and coldest he had ever experienced, and his letters confirmed it. In one from August 1951, he speaks of having only "light attacks" from the enemy, and that, "Our mortars killed and wounded about 30 of them yesterday." Yet, in the next paragraph, he says he's sorry to hear that Martha Jean's husband, Bob, did not like his job much. "I don't like mine very much, either," he wrote, "but mine won't be over for the next couple of years… Tell Bob he's going to have to get himself a hardware store in Terre Haute or Clinton and work for himself before he will be satisfied."

In one of my favorite passages, he wrote: "I have been sitting here listening to Jack Benny, Red Skelton, Phil Harris, and 'Amos 'n Andy' on the radio…The boys [in his outfit] seem to spend lots of hours with alcohol and women. I often wonder how they will look back at their actions when their kids grow up."

Gib's skill with radios eventually made him a pretty important man in his unit. Not only did he maintain its telephone lines and equipment (becoming a target for enemy snipers along the way), but he also made a steady number of friends, and a little extra income, by fixing everyone else's radios; his letters often include lists of badly-needed radio tubes. He wrote that despite living in a hillside dugout, he had rigged a decent stove, and he rarely lacked friends, either: "I got a pretty nice home," he wrote on a chilly October night in 1951. "…my radio is working fine, so I have company, sometimes when I don't want it, especially about bed-time."

In one of the most telling passages I read, Gib wrote of being pulled back from the front for good, and it looked as though he would be coming home without ever having to go near a battle again; it was February 1952. It had been "cold and windy," and he suffered through nighttime guard duty. But before he closed his letter, he wrote: "I was talking to a North Korean prisoner the other day, and he said he was a Christian. He knew several church hymns. He said he was drafted by the communists when the war started. It has been three years since he was home with his folks, so I guess my situation could be worse."

My father-in-law's letters have helped teach me once again that there's more to war than recognizing heroes and medals and generals and battlefield glory. It is often about a lonely man who is trying to stay warm and clean and fed; it's about missing a family or a sweetheart; it's about wanting more than anything else the ordinary life of a farm or a small-town Friday night. It's about wanting—perhaps more than anything else—to go home.

In a letter dated December 1, 1951, Gib wrote that the "fighting has just about come to a standstill. We aren't shooting at them, and they aren't shooting at us. We just sit on our respective hills and watch each other while the wheels argue about the big question. I'll believe it when they sign it."

Of course, the war went on…

A Prayer for Casper

November 23, 2015

We have a sharing time at our small church every Sunday in which anyone in our congregation can speak up, whether it be about a concern or a sickness, a stroke of good fortune or joy. It is a tradition with those of us there, an act of easy-going ecclesiastical democracy that's been in place as long as there's been a building in which to meet, a hymn to sing, or a sermon to be heard.

Since there aren't that many of us there, I suppose we all have taken our turns over the years, announcing the births of our children and grandchildren, the challenges our friends and family members have faced in illnesses and hard times, and in giving thanks for the blessings of cards and flowers that we've gotten just when we needed them most.

Last January, we sat for a while and listened to the travails of Sara Edwards, who, like all of us, feels that "sharing time" is not just a phrase we use, but something we mean.

Sara, who is about the same age as my wife and me, has experienced many of life's transitions at about the same time as we have, and since we have always had animals and pets in our world, we understood when Sara sometimes spoke about hers. On that particular Sunday, something was weighing so heavily on her that she decided to speak about it: she needed prayers for a cat named Ted.

Of course, Sara told the story with tears in her eyes, but that's understandable, for Ted—which Sara did not own, and was watching for a friend, Tammy Wilson—had pulled off an escape from her Clinton home as deftly as a World War II stalag inmate after months of planning. So, Sara, upset that she had let Ted pull a Houdini, and exhausted after days of searching for him, was asking for prayers to go up for Ted's return. And, I think they did.

To make a long story a little bit shorter, it turned out well for Ted, but not before Sarah also got involved in something right out of an *I Love Lucy* episode. Lucy—I mean, Sara—went through her neighborhood by car and on foot, hoping Ted would be so scared he'd run back into her arms as soon as he heard her voice. It didn't quite work out that way…

For a few more fevered days after she had shared her story with us, Sara fretted and hunted, combing her neighborhood as if on an FBI manhunt, and, lo and behold, she finally found Ted sitting under a parked car a block from her house. She coaxed him out and promptly took him home to feed; then she let Tammy know that Ted was back from his excellent adventure, no worse for wear.

However, when the tabby's owner came to Sara's house for a joyful reunion, she immediately told our relieved friend that the cat she had jubilantly returned home with was, in fact, not Ted, but a Ted look-a-like, an imposter, who must be owned by someone else, for he looked well-fed. Plunged back into despair, Sara now realized that her problems had been compounded: she had taken someone else's cat; she was a catnapper. Since she had no Ethel Mertz to do her dirty work, Sara discovered and returned Ted II to its rightful owner, Alicia Frazier, who thought the whole thing was funny.

Ted did return in early February; Sara opened her door, and there he sat, looking at her with a slight grin on his face that suggested he had enjoyed yanking her emotional chain. When Sara turned Ted over to Tammy, she says she had a warm feeling that all those prayers on Ted's behalf must have worked, and that should have been that. But, it isn't.

With no small amount of irony, Sara was given a cat in June by none other than Alicia Frazier. It wasn't Ted Jr., or Son of Ted, but it was a beautiful little kitten that Sara's four grandchildren called Casper. "He's a very friendly guy, …purring all the time," Sara says.

A month ago, it was Casper's turn to go AWOL, and a week later, Sara spoke up again during sharing, and told us once more about a cat that she hopes will return. One minute Casper was there, and the next Sara was thinking about making posters she could staple to neighborhood telephone poles and mini-mart bulletin boards. Now, she just wants Casper home, and as was the case for the biblical "prodigal son," no questions will be asked as to what riotous living he's been up to.

"The thing is," Sara says, "I keep believing that he's going to show up; I haven't lost faith. Our granddaughters (Olivia, Sophie, Everly, and Dylyn) have helped me walk to the neighbors and knock on doors. They believe he's going to come back, too."

So, with tears in her eyes, Sara is hopeful that her friends at church will pray for Casper's safe return. As of this past week, however, he had not come home.

Sometimes these things take time.

A Reminder That History Is Important

December 7, 2015

A story related by the Canadian historian Margaret MacMillan in her book, *Dangerous Games: The Uses and Abuses of History*, tells of American writer Sarah Jacoby overhearing a barroom conversation on the evening of Sept. 11, 2001.

"This is just like Pearl Harbor," one man says.

"What is Pearl Harbor?" his friend asks.

"That's when the Vietnamese dropped bombs on a harbor, and it started the Vietnam War," the first man replies.

Today is Pearl Harbor Day, the 74th anniversary of the "date that will live in infamy," when Japanese forces precipitated America's entry into World War II with a surprise attack on our naval base in Hawaii. I'd hate to think that the accuracy of the history the storyteller inflicted upon his drinking buddy—whether he'd had a few too many drinks or not—represents just how little Americans know about the subject, but I'm afraid it may very well be so.

MacMillan asks the readers of her essay if it even matters that the pair got their history so wrong, but quickly answers her own question: "I would argue that it does, that a citizenry that has so little knowledge of the past cannot begin to put the present into context, can too easily be fed stories by those who claim to speak with the knowledge of history and its lessons."

I teach American History, and I have similar fears, particularly in a year when so much political rhetoric fills the airwaves. It is, as well, yet another year of even more debate about what is perceived as the sad state of American secondary education. But the fact is we don't value our history as much as we should, and we value it as a subject in our schools even less, partly because state mandates force us to focus on the inanity of school grades and the like. History, and courses such as Citizenship and Civics, have, for the most part, taken a seat in the back of the educational bus as the mania of standardized tests engulfs us.

All the while, our history lessons—that which is perceived as being dusty and dead and housed between the leather-bound covers of yellowing library books—continue to take it on the chin.

Losing our sense of history is more than simply getting a few important dates or facts confused during a tough episode of *Jeopardy* at dinnertime. History is one subject—perhaps above all others, save literature—that can help us gain a sense of appreciation, not only for what we have, but also for those who fought to help us get and keep it. What happened at Pearl Harbor, and in the subsequent war—the greatest conflict in world history—is important, even to those who are bored with the study of it.

"When the world is storm-driven and the bad that happens and the worse that threatens are so urgent as to shut out everything else from view, then we need to know all the strong fortresses of the spirit which men have built through the ages," historian David McCullough said in a lecture delivered a dozen years ago. That seems to apply to the world we are living in right now...

Dr. Don Layton, professor emeritus at Indiana State University and author of *World War II: A Global Perspective,* made history exciting for me in the years I sat in three of his courses at ISU. He's concerned that the subject is underappreciated, as well.

"We would be much the worse off if we did not know history," Layton says. "History helps us understand those with whom we have to deal, and it helps us understand ourselves. It encourages people in the present to reflect on themselves. History helps us understand other people's values, fears, hopes, and how they are likely to react to something we do. It shows us that it is wrong to assume other people are just like you. That was certainly the problem at Pearl Harbor."

On the morning of December 7, 1941, a force of 350 Japanese airplanes attacked the American naval base in hopes of wiping out the U.S. Pacific Fleet; over

2,400 Americans lost their lives, nearly half going down with the USS Arizona. The Oklahoma also sank, and seven other ships were badly damaged, while hundreds of aircraft were also lost. The plan may very well have been steeped in the study by Japan's top military planners of other such attacks in history; the British had carried out such a raid in Italy just a year before.

"The Japanese did not think as we in the West did," Layton says. "Pearl Harbor was the result of a vast combination of interrelated, complicated historical factors, false assumptions, and fallacious views. Nothing takes place in a vacuum. Events flow out of one another in an unending stream, and history can aid in deciphering that flow.

"The Japanese attack was more than one of the most daring and brilliant naval operations of all time; it was one of the turning points in history. What began with the Japanese attack at Pearl Harbor ended with mushroom clouds over Hiroshima and Nagasaki. We have lived under these clouds ever since. Yet, what happened at Pearl Harbor is one of the greatest of all war stories. It combined so much, so suddenly, so unexpectedly, in such brief and tragic compass. That, plus the bravery of the men who fought and died there are compelling reasons to study Pearl Harbor and not to exclude it from our historical memory," Layton added.

Near the end of his speech, McCullough goes on to tell us, "History teaches that nothing happens in isolation, or without cause and effect, and that nothing ever had to happen as it did... History is about change, because the world has never not been changing, indeed because life itself is change."

I could leave this piece with philosopher George Santayana's famous line that, "Those who do not remember the past are condemned to repeat it." It seems more appropriate, however, on this Pearl Harbor Day, to quote Calvin Coolidge. He said, "The nation which forgets its defenders will itself be forgotten."

Now I Know What I Want for Christmas

December 21, 2015

My son called a few days ago and wanted to know if I "had any ideas" about what I wanted for Christmas. It wasn't the first time he's asked.

Evan has been after me since mid-November to give him just one thing I'd like to find under the tree, but I couldn't think of anything. Really.

My kids have become frustrated with their parents and Christmas gifts. It seems we have just about everything we want or have room to keep, so we usually put them off by telling them we'll "…think of something soon," then get busy doing anything but.

The noise of mall "musak" wafted in the background of Evan's call and suggested to me that he was braving the madness of Christmas shopping right then.

Because I know he hates shopping nearly as much as I do, I figured he wanted to deal with my gift while he was already caught up in the maelstrom of it all. I just needed to give him one gleam of hope, but I couldn't.

The problem is that his mother and I really don't know what we want for Christmas, other than pictures of our grandson. Joanie wants a new can opener, but, of course, that is a terrible gift to open on Christmas morning; I think I'd rather unwrap underwear than a can opener. I don't want to be the kind of man who gives his wife a can opener for Christmas; I'm not Leroy Lockhorn.

About the time they were our ages, my parents used to tell us three kids that they didn't need anything, either, and I always moaned that there would never be a time when I didn't have a list of things ready, but I've apparently been proven wrong.

Joanie used to keep a list so I wouldn't "surprise" her with clothes I had picked out on my own in my annual Christmas Eve shopping frenzy. That dazed and confused last-minute marathon is a common ritual among the American male, for I see other mumbling husbands wandering the mall with furrowed brows in search of their wives' gifts, too.

Joanie has always been too polite to tell me when something I've chosen for her is not to her liking, so we came to an understanding years ago that what I bought her usually "wouldn't fit" and would need to be returned. But we don't even play that game anymore; I won't buy her any clothes now, unless it's a sweatshirt or socks.

I eventually told Evan that I'd have to get back with him. "I can't think of anything I want, son. Your mom and I are buying each other kayaks this year; maybe we'll need something for them," I said, suspecting that he was, at that moment, picturing his parents dunked and paddleless along the Big Raccoon next summer. "Maybe I can use a flashlight," I finally told him. "A flashlight would be good enough," I said.

"Okay, what else?" he responded, and that's when I told him I had to go to the bathroom.

Christmas lists were easier to make when we were kids. I imagine that just about everyone who's my age remembers the huge Sears and Roebuck *Christmas Wishbook* we got each year. I usually discovered ours in late October, and from that time—through the approximate life sentence I had to serve before Christmas morning finally came—I would sit at the kitchen table or lie in my bunk bed and thumb through the massive toy section of that 600-page catalog. On those inviting, glistening pages I saw and slobbered over erector sets, G.I. Joes, basketballs, and bicycles. With each turn, I found chemistry sets, Sears Elevator Service centers, and All-State electric trains. For years, I wanted a "Flatliner" bike, one that had "a 'Bendix' coaster brake, jet fins, white-walled tires, and a dual-beam headlight."

I also wanted a Lionel "Daredevil Road Race" slot car set, just like the one my cousin, Roger, set up in his bedroom. The *Wishbook* made that seem possible, even though I knew that my parents couldn't afford a fraction of the toys I dreamed of.

A few evenings back, I sat at my writing desk, thinking I would love to get my hands on one of those catalogs again. Since just about everything else can be found on the web, I decided to see if I could find one, and I did at WishbookWeb.com. It features thousands of scanned pages from dozens of catalogs, some reaching back as far as the 1930s.

I eventually found what I longed for in the 1964 edition, and it didn't take much imagination to see myself again in those days, impossibly skinny with a crew cut and in patched J.C. Penney blue jeans, poring through an inconceivable array of toys. On page 166, I found something I knew I wanted back then: a "Paratrooper Jumpmaster," a 22-piece set of "authentic fighting gear." The action-filled tagline read: "You've buried your 'chute.' Now set out on your mission with your 19-inch Tommy gun…" The set included grenades, a machete and compass, even a field pack and ration box; it cost a whopping $5.99.

I spent over an hour looking through the catalog that day, grinning, I'm sure, when I found the Fort Apache set that I played with for years; its tagline imploring me to "protect the stockade against Indian attack." I found the black fiberboard telescope my brother, John, and I shared, exploring the moon from our flat rooftop. I found our bow-and-arrow set and BB gun, and the Fred Flintstone vinyl punching bag that took one too many shots to the head.

But on page 168 of the *Wishbook*, I saw something

that really caught my eye, as it had when I was 8 years old: a "Paladin, 'Have Gun Will Travel' Set," complete with calling cards, double, knight-laden black holsters, and a pair of ivory-handled pistols. All the set really lacked was Richard Boone, himself. On the same page were similar sets with "Bonanza" and "Roy Rogers" themes, and I was assured that with any of them I would have been able to "slap leather, lightning fast."

I don't live in the past, but I sure don't mind going there every once in a while. In the meantime, I have to come up with something that my son and daughter can give to me on Christmas morning. Too bad it's not 1964.

The Cat That Came in from the Cold

January 18, 2016

I have written about our old orange tabby cat, Max, in other stories; he was a part of our lives well before I ever began to occupy this space on the newspaper's front page and, with continued luck, will be with us a while still.

Max is nearly 16 now, an unusually long life for a country cat that has taken his daily chances roaming the woods, sleeping in possum and raccoon-filled quarters, and eating things we'd rather not even think about. He's survived close scrapes with speeding cars and carnivorous coyotes and territorial tom cats over all that time, and must be, despite evidence to the contrary, a fairly wily old guy.

Originally my son's pet, Max was once energetic and relatively well-groomed. He started his life with us indoors, that is until we'd had enough of his failure to grasp even rudimentary litter box training. He was eventually banned from the house, first to the garage, then to a life sentence in and around our barn.

He has no discerning taste whatsoever when it comes to hiking his leg, and so, despite having a lovable and docile nature—and being neutered in an attempt to remedy the problem—Max's overactive bladder has kept him from joining our family's inner circle.

For years, I found him maddeningly dim-witted. For example, he has managed to get himself locked in my tool shop, our mini-barn, and my truck; he refuses to drink clean water from an often-scrubbed pan I keep near our hydrant, preferring to quench his thirst by awkwardly contorting himself to reach the shallow bowl of a flower garden St. Joseph statue.

He somehow manages to get his tail slammed in a door on a weekly basis, just one of the reasons that the appendage is about half the length it once was. If there is a way he can work his way between my legs when I have my hands full, he'll do it. Of course, he also just loves to see the siding of our house wet.

Yet Max has become somewhat synonymous with our homestead. His irritating chalkboard-scrape of a voice is the first thing we most often hear when opening a car door upon arriving home. Because we've always seen his now-stubby tail bobbing along in front of the garage door as soon as our headlights illuminate the house, we have always imagined that he was on patrol 24 hours a day. But we now realize that as he's aged, Max requires about 18 of his hours in the sack, his youthful vigilance taking a back seat to a warm bed.

Whether he knows it or not, Joanie and I have always looked out for Max's best interests. I have chased off aggressive rivals, have installed a cozy heat lamp atop his roomy and warm pet bed in the barn, and have seen to it that he's been fed twice a day (not including his after-school snack), and I don't think his rarely used water dish has ever been empty.

Joanie has invested even more time on his behalf. She has never allowed him to miss an appointment with the corps of veterinarians that has kept him vaccinated and treated for whatever ailed him. Over the years, I know my wife has poked enough pills down, given enough shots to, and rubbed enough medication on Max that he should never be so ungrateful as to even consider hosing down a car tire or potted plant again.

But this year, like an old man who is decidedly set in his ways, Max no longer wants to sleep in our barn on even the coldest nights, preferring instead to perch atop a stack of firewood outside our door. After two or three weeks of seeing him there—his head popping up like a prairie dog's every time we walked past the window—I realized he wasn't straying from that spot for hardly a minute. Like Melville's "Bartleby the Scrivener," Max had come to stay in a most inconvenient spot.

It didn't take long to find the reason either: A vagrant tom cat has taken to raiding Max's bowl, and the old man (he's nearing 80 in human years), once the king of his forest (can you hear Bert Lahr singing?), is letting the rude newcomer have his way. I think Max knows he's too old to fight anymore.

Because his rival has been a bit too elusive to catch when we've had the time to haul him to the local shelter—and I can't stand to think that he's hungry too—I began to feed Max near our back garage door, and then even closer yet to his lofty wooden perch near the window.

Real winter weather arrived last week, so I first put down blankets on the wood to make him more comfortable, then added a pet bed, then a heated pad to keep him warm. But cold winds and blowing rains threatened to make his new digs miserable too, and I told Joanie, "I think we're going to have to start bringing Max in at night. He'll freeze."

Of course, that's what we're doing, and just in time because we are expecting, as I write this, lows in single digits. So Max, that once independent loner, that killer of chipmunks, that boss of the barn and fearless night watchman, ambles through our garage door to bed down on a blanket near our upright freezer and recycling cans; we are hopeful he'll use his own litter box.

He has, nearly overnight, become dependent on us. Like the old man of a cat he is, he's accepting a hand to get out of his chair, will allow someone else to hold a door for him, particularly if they get his tail out of the way before it closes.

I can't say that our relationship over the years with Max has always been smooth, but he's ours. May he stay warm; may he catch mice in his dreams.

Nameless, Unremembered Acts of Kindness

January 25, 2016

A teaching friend of mine, Clay Huffman, surprised nearly everyone in our gymnasium a few days ago when he sank a dramatic half-court shot to claim a $100 prize. What seventh-grader Lindsey Peterson did with the money he'd won amazed everyone even more.

Here's the backstory: Lindsey's name was drawn during a homecoming pep session for a chance to win the cash. She was given a choice: either shoot a half-court shot herself or choose a teacher to do it. Because almost every nuclear-lunged kid in the gym was chanting Huffman's name (the guy looks like he can bench press a Buick and wear out a treadmill), Lindsey opted for the popular coach who teaches her physical education class every sixth block. He promptly drilled the shot from about 45 feet.

Then—if you're ready for this—that slender, soft-spoken, long-haired kid with a shy smile and braces on her teeth, a young girl who in so many ways is typical of the kids we so often are told are self-absorbed and can't find their priorities with a telescope—told our principal, Kyle Kersey, that she wanted to give the money to the school's Sarah Norton Scholarship Fund. The big guy just about cried.

Sarah was a popular teacher and administrator at our school; she died last fall after losing her fight with cancer. Lindsey hardly knew Norton, but it seems she hardly needed to.

It's ironic, but I talked to Lindsey the day following her simple act of kindness, having not yet heard what she'd done with her winnings. Because I do a little writing and picture taking for the school, I did what I've always done a week ago Saturday: attended our annual winter homecoming game.

I enjoy homecomings (we have one in the fall, too). I get to talk to the "kids" I had years ago, and in many cases, they are the parents of the kids I have now. I also snap a few pictures of the homecoming king and queen for the newspapers, eat too much food that, with my aging arteries considered, should be left alone, and generally have a good time, particularly if we happen to win a ballgame.

So that's where you would have found me that night: planted in the upper-level gym seats at about midcourt, shoveling down nachos and popcorn like I was at a Super Bowl party, and watching what turned out to be an exciting game.

Before I headed down to the floor to squeeze into the paparazzi of proud parents, cheerleaders, and students, who also wanted to get pictures of the newly named royalty, I sat with my wife and a few of our former students. As we talked, I got a little carried away with a loaded nacho and managed to drip a small dab of melted cheese on a young girl in front of me. I apologized, handed her a napkin to mop up the mess on her sweatshirt, and was reminded by a friend that the girl, just the day before, had been the one who'd won the $100 prize at our pep session; she could afford a new sweatshirt. I congratulated her for her windfall and made my way down the stairs with my camera.

Lindsey hasn't been at our school before this year. I couldn't have recalled her name a year or two ago, but I do know her mother, Brandy, who teaches reading at one of our elementary schools. In fact, I used to see Lindsey there as Joanie and I walked the hallways for exercise on the coldest winter days. Lindsey nearly always had her nose in a book, often while she followed her mom obediently up the hallway to head for home.

After I learned of Lindsey's generosity, I asked her why she gave her winnings away; surely a seventh-grader has a few hundred things in mind to buy. Without batting one of those timid eyes of hers, she said, "I told Mr. Kersey I just didn't need the money."

Most readers who follow my stories know that I am a part-time writer and a full-time teacher. I can't help but let the latter job mix with the former, and so every once in a while, I tell you about a student or a teacher who has made me proud to be doing what I do for a living. What Lindsey did reflects the way she's been raised; it silently shouts out about the character and generosity we rarely give our kids the credit for having.

I likely won't still be teaching by the time Lindsey is old enough to sit in one of my classes, but if she ever does, she'll probably hear me read a few lines from one of my favorite poets, William Wordsworth. In his "Lines Written A Few Miles Above Tintern Abbey," he says: "the best portion of a good man's life" is his "little, nameless, unremembered acts of kindness and love."

Apparently you don't need to be a man—or even be out of junior high school—to already know that.

A Lesson Even a 4th Grader Can Understand

February 15, 2016

Being a schoolteacher, I have to admit that one of the reasons I appreciate today being Presidents Day is that I won't have to crawl out of bed this morning at 5:30 to head to work. Our birds and cats will have to wait until after sunup for breakfast, something that only they will see as tragic.

Although we take Presidents Day off, the students and teachers in my district attend school on Veterans Day and Martin Luther King Day; many undoubtedly wish they had those days off, too. But we come to school not only to extend our summers a few days, but also because we feel it's best to be learning something in our convocations and classroom lessons.

Yet Presidents Day means a break on which we can depend—unless we are making up a snow day—

during the dreary weeks of midwinter, and I must say that it comes at just the right time.

Unless I am mistaken, we used to take both the birthdays of President Lincoln (February 12) and President Washington (the 22nd) off in my elementary school days. We'd color posters of an axe-wielding Abe and wooden-toothed George, and listen to mostly embellished but inspirational stories about wrestling matches and cherry trees. Of course, Lincoln's presidency had barely ended by the time I entered grade school; at least, that's what my students probably think.

Presidents Day—a holiday created in 1971 by the Uniform Monday Holiday Act—was part of an attempt to create more 3-day weekends for federal workers. Originally observed as Washington's birthday, it was celebrated as a national holiday starting in 1885, but today we supposedly recognize the importance of all our past presidents on this third Monday in February; yes, even Millard Fillmore.

The holiday does suffer a lack of respect, for it is often seen as little more than an opportunity for a good white sale or mark-down on "all major appliances." Unfortunately, Washington and Lincoln collectively have become cardboard cutouts and mountainside effigies to us, lost amid the tide of political correctness and revisionist history.

But in this particular election year, with its debate-filled posturing and campaign-driven bloviation, I think we'd be better off if we paid a little more attention to what that dynamic presidential duo still has to say to us, and how they said it.

I recently read an article from last October's *Esquire Magazine* written by Jack Holmes. In it, he explains how the *Boston Globe* used an algorithm, known as the "Flesch-Kincaid Readability Test," to measure the "complexity levels of a speaker's diction." The test "theoretically concludes the level of education an average person would need to have in order to understand it." They applied the test to the speeches of the then-19 presidential candidates, and I don't suppose it comes as much of a surprise that virtually none of the contenders were speaking at the complexity level required of high school sophomores. Atop the list is Jim Gilmore, who dropped out of the race just last Friday; he addressed his faithful at the 10th grade level, while Donald Trump, who has one of the largest followings, brought up the rear at fourth grade. Most of the other contenders fell in the middle school range.

I'm not making a political endorsement here, nor taking a cheap shot at any candidate or party. In fact, I have to say that speaking at a level that everyone can understand is usually a good thing, but I also find it dangerous, and a bit depressing, that we as a people have come to simply accept the hucksterism of the 30-second soundbite as the best we can get.

Washington virtually created the presidency; what the Constitution's second article did not state about the newly-created office, he initiated through precedent. Above all, Washington understood power—

its uses and abuses. He knew he could have reigned nearly as a king, yet he made his decision to serve no more than two terms, a remarkable thing really. Despite the fact that few Americans in the late 18th century had formal educations, he also chose to speak and write at levels decidedly higher than the fourth grade.

At once, Washington also saw the evils of party politics, and addressed them at length in his farewell address, which was first published in newspapers, and then in pamphlets in September 1796. He wrote: "The alternate domination of one faction over another, sharpened by the spirit of revenge, natural to party dissension, which in different ages and countries has perpetrated the most horrid enormities, is itself a frightful despotism. But this leads at length to a more formal and permanent despotism. The disorders and miseries which result gradually incline the minds of men to seek security and repose in the absolute power of an individual."

I was recently reminded of a story about England's King George III. Upon learning that Washington had decided to leave the presidency behind and retire to his farm, the king supposedly said, "If he does that, he will be the greatest man in the world." Of course, Washington did do it.

Lincoln, who had virtually no formal schooling, nonetheless taught himself to write and speak through the cadences and rhythms of the *King James Bible* and in everything Shakespeare wrote. In what I believe is the greatest speech in our history, his Second Inaugural, which he delivered on March 4, 1865, to an audience composed mostly of common citizens (including John Wilkes Booth, who killed him a few weeks later), Lincoln taught an even greater lesson still: forgiveness and reunification.

With what has been said to be a voice higher than expected for such a large man, he said, "With malice toward none, with charity for all, with firmness in the right as God gives us to see the right, let us strive on to finish the work we are in, to bind up the nation's wounds, to care for him who shall have borne the battle and for his widow and his orphan, to do all which may achieve and cherish a just and lasting peace among ourselves and with all nations."

When I re-read these and other words from Washington and Lincoln, I realize again why we should be celebrating their births, and it's for reasons other than having a day off or finding linens at a good price.

In this winter of our political discontent, we need to be reminded that their greatness was not created 30 seconds at a time, that leadership isn't merely upsmanship, and that real statesmen do more than just talk.

Let There Be Light Over the Kitchen Table

February 29, 2016

Far from being the kind of guy who subscribes to *Handyman* magazine or feels comfortable in conversations about tools much more complicated than a hammer, I do, nonetheless, like to be sure that what I own works. So when our 30-year-old kitchen ceiling light quit working last week, I knew I'd soon be sticking my nose into its sockets and wiring, whether I knew what I was doing or not.

Joanie feels I sell myself way too short when it comes to home maintenance projects, and perhaps I do, but the last thing I want is to be the man neighbors whisper about following his poor electrical job gone wrong, his do-it-yourself but lop-sided roof, his ruinous plumbing that would have cost half as much had he just called a professional. Since I had already had success in recent days in repairing a broken sweeper cord and a balky microwave oven switch, I figured that I couldn't break the light much worse than it already was.

On the appointed day after work, I came home in the late afternoon with such purpose that I didn't bother to change into my requisite sloppy jeans and T-shirt. I simply flipped the circuit breaker to the ceiling lights off, grabbed my flashlight and a screwdriver, and went to work, a kitchen table chair serving me as a ladder.

What I found was a bit disheartening: the wiring in the light in question (there are two others sitting just under a four-bladed ceiling fan) appeared to be charred, the insulation crusty, some of it breaking off in my fingers. The connections holding the wire to the back of the ceramic socket were loose and a bit burned, too, and the only way they were going to work like new involved soldering, which usually looks easier than it really is.

Without going into any of the technical language (I really don't know it anyway), I came away from the initial exploratory surgery feeling that I needed to replace or trim the old wiring, then attach it to a new socket. But I first tried cleaning up the wire, applying a bit of electrical tape to it, then re-assembling the housing. Declaring, "Let there be light!" as I snapped the breaker back on, it was instantly obvious there'd be no miracle.

By the time I had the light back together the first time, it was after 5 p.m., and I knew that the closest hardware store was closed. So I did the most practical thing, and it wasn't to simply wait until I could get the right parts. Instead, I called my buddy, Joe, who has—if I might say euphemistically—a lot of stuff in his shop... Picking up on the second ring, Joe said he did have a ceramic socket that I could use and that he'd find it and come right up, probably because he thought of my skills as an electrician first, and secondly because he thought I could use a hand.

Before he ever made it from his truck to the door, I knew that Joe had misunderstood what I needed; he brought a ceramic fixture that had a socket and pull chain built into it—about what I have wired into my barn. Laying that on the table, he watched as I took the light fixture apart again, and soon concurred that soldering the old socket wouldn't be worth it. He promptly volunteered to drive me to the nearest open hardware store, and off we went, that is after he called his wife, Linda, to tell her not to wait on him for supper. It's a true friend who will miss supper to go to the hardware store, but Joe sees copper tubing and toilet seats and deck screws like Audrey Hepburn did a Tiffany's showcase, so I believed him when he said he wanted to go.

It is on those kinds of trips—to and from some hardware store or lumber yard or mechanical supply—that Joe and I have become such good friends, I think. Since he retired from teaching, it is on home projects and at the occasional restaurant table that we now share news about our families and gab about our friends. And that is what we did as we dodged potholes on the way to town and back.

Forty-five minutes later, we were home to the dark kitchen that Joanie had given up on, since we'd be bumping into one another like bad dance partners had she started dinner for us. She disappeared to the other end of the house, and Joe took up his position as flashlight holder while I snipped wiring and installed the new socket.

After I'd finished, my God-like muttering failed again upon flipping the breaker, but Joe agreed when I suggested that we should have checked the connections for all the light's wires, since we had undoubtedly loosened things up a bit with all our tugging and wire-stripping. Removing a few stubborn screws and making careful inspection of the intestines of wiring farther up into the light must have done the trick; we had light a quarter-of-an-hour later.

It was well past 7 pm by the time Joe and I had finished our conversation and tool collecting, and he headed for home. Once again, the same lights that have shown down above our kitchen table since the days my daughter was in a crib and Cabbage Patch Kids came out, since the first mobile telephones came on the market and a gallon of milk was $1, were burning bright.

It may sound a bit old-fashioned to say it, but while Joanie started supper, I thought about all the time we'd spent under that light—the 4H projects and meals, the arm-wrestling and coffee sipping, the newspaper reading and prayers and homework…

What's a few hours of work compared to those things?

A Month for Libraries and Reading

April 11, 2016

I had as wonderful a spring vacation as one can have without it involving beach sand and suntan lotion. I worked in my yard in shirt sleeves, walked most days with Joanie, ate good food with good friends, slept until I wanted to get out of bed, and read each night until my chin drooped.

Reading books is an essential part of what and who I am, and it is absolutely incomprehensible when someone says they don't read much because they don't have the patience for it. To me, that's like saying that they've lost patience with breathing; I wish books meant more to people these days.

April is a month in which literacy and reading and poetry are celebrated. It is, for instance, "National Poetry Month" and "School Library Month." The week of April 10-16 is "National Library Week," and tomorrow is "Library Workers Day," which makes perfect sense to me since I give my favorite librarian a hug every day.

April 12 is also "Drop Everything and Read Day," a celebration that I hope we all observe, particularly in our schools. Perhaps we actually need to start calling it, "Put Down Your Phone or Laptop and Read Day," because it is our preoccupation with both that seems to have led to more books becoming dust collectors. April 13 is "National Bookmobile Day," too; I'll have more to say about that in a minute.

And, I guess I was too busy tending to other things to let you know in last month's stories that March was "National Reading Month," but, oh, how I celebrated that; I think I may still have a bit of a reading hangover.

I fear for reading in our country. Not only do I believe there is an assault on the pure pleasure of learning things in our "culture," but I also think there is a growing aversion to it. Storing facts and ideas and memorizations in our own gray matter is still a pretty useful thing, yet we are teaching our children that knowing things is a secondary skill to looking them up on the Internet, that what they need to know is only a "Google" search away. It is an unfortunate development, one we are paying for every time we require a calculator to figure a simple tip at dinner, a GPS to know what direction in which we are headed, or struggle with reading material that requires us to use allusions and historical references that we no longer learn or know. I honestly believe that our national literacy is up for grabs. We had better use it or lose it.

I am concerned that although we are doing a pretty good job of showing kids how to read words, they are developing huge gaps in what they should know and remember. Our kids aren't reading enough literature, enough poetry and short stories and novels and history. Instead, they are spending less and less time with books as they age, and part of the fault lies in that we are not emphasizing the joy and pure pleasure of reading good books to them. After all, there are so many things for children and teachers to do with their time, like preparing for standardized tests, which, the way I see it, compartmentalizes and minimizes what they "need to know."

I always thought that our knowledge should reach across disciplines; my favorite writers all do that. I have to add that I find no comfort in recent promises to rid our kids of the scourge of ISTEP; the powers that be will get it repackaged as "new and improved," and the madness and money will continue to flow.

Not everyone has the time to slow down long enough to read much; I am, for instance, aware of what has happened to my own free time, and to that of my son and daughter-in-law before they had my grandson to tend to; my wife manages to read for pleasure only during vacations. But we should be making time in school for our kids to read, and much of that time should be spent reading what they want to read, and reading good books that their teachers have read and have recommended to them. We should be talking to our kids about books all the time, and we should be encouraging them to talk about them, too.

I'm unrealistic enough to believe that every minute our children spend looking at computerized reading programs in school should be matched with free reading time, reading for the fun of reading. And I'm not just putting the onus on schools, either. What has replaced reading in many of our homes? The satellite television program guide?

That is where the bookmobile and public libraries came into play for me. My elementary school had no library—although we did have plenty of books in our classrooms—but among the fondest memories of my early days come from the times we were allowed out of class to walk hand-in-hand with our teachers to the branch public library in North Terre Haute. Wandering the library's creaking old floorboards was a great adventure for us; we never knew what we'd find among all those books. How many great reads would I have missed had I only searched an online catalogue for a few titles?

On other occasions, we stepped into the "Bookmobile" that regularly visited the school. I had little else in my wallet (my leathercraft-made church camp wallet) in those days but a blue library card, and I remember that I checked out a book on World War I and its heroes so often that I was told by the librarian that I'd have to let other children have a chance to read it before I could take it again.

Books are not dead; they live and breathe. Printed words on paper are not static; they are not stationary bikes on which we work up a sweat but go nowhere; they are not boats in a harbor with furled sails. The poet Emily Dickinson wrote that "There is no frigate like a book," and I believe her. Our libraries should be revered places, special places, starting places for great adventures.

In just a few years, my grandson, Daniel, will be reading; his librarian grandmother and writer grandpa will be more than happy to see to it that he has all the books he can handle. If it is a book he wants, I will buy it.

Daniel Handler—better known as Lemony Snicket—says, "A good library will never be too neat, or too dusty, because somebody will always be in it, taking books off the shelves and staying up late reading them."

I so hope that is true.

Duffing with Dudley and the Boys

May 9, 2016

It is about this time of year each spring that three old teaching buddies and I make an annual golf pilgrimage to the southern part of the state. We are occasional golfers, Sam and Sheldon, Dudley and me, but we got into the habit years ago of packing and going, so we've just kept to tradition. We have grown too stubborn to give up on what has usually become one day of golf, one day of watching it rain, and two days of peace and quiet for our wives.

As the youngest in the quartet, I am the only one that still has to show up for work each day, but since I have enough personal time built up to last Methuselah, I make the reservations, and off we go.

We used to leave the organizing up to Sam, but he once booked Sheldon and me into a room with a single bed. I think the world of Sheldon, but since I have also seen *Planes, Trains, and Automobiles,* I slept on a hotel couch. It turned out to be a bed only a masochist could love, so since then—and I suspect Sam wanted it that way in the first place—I have made all the arrangements.

It is ritual for Sam and Sheldon to meet at my place before we head south for 45 minutes or so to pick up Dudley. It has also become customary to drive a while before we stop to eat breakfast. After filling our tanks with cholesterol, sugars, and caffeine, we drive another 90 minutes south, catching up on each others' lives as we amble down the road.

Since I do the driving, I am usually the first to notice Sam's nodding head in the rearview mirror. The conversation is then shared three ways instead of four until he regains consciousness.

Dudley is the best golfer in the group, the kind of player that others call to fill out a foursome, particularly if there is money to be won. The rest of us have our moments, but, for the most part, we wallow in inconsistency—a birdie and great shot here, a "worm burner" and double bogey there, and since we are too sedate now to toss clubs and rant, we vent our ire by muttering under our breaths quite a bit. We play for no money, and actually encourage one another (although my secret goal in life is to beat Dudley); why, the other three even trust me with the scorecard.

The British probably invented the term, "to duff." It is, among several other things—including one's own posterior—a verb that describes one of golf's greatest sins: to abuse the turf in front of a golf ball, an act that results in a dribbling shot that struggles to make it past the ladies' tees. Since we all have been known to commit the error—even Dudley indulges, but rarely—I have taken to calling our gang of four "The Old Duffers."

A few years back, we met every week over the summer to play and had great fun doing it, despite an uncanny knack for meeting on days when the temperatures soared above 90. It is amazing, really, that grown men will traipse around on scorched hillsides and in mosquito-infested miasmas, sweat dripping into their eyes, all the while paying for their discomfort, but that is one of the many inexplicable things about golf. And we usually do it, as Dave Barry says, while wearing "bad clothing."

On this recent trip, we played a course on the first day that included a lot of water. I told Sam about it ahead of time, so he packed a few extra gross of golf balls, including just about every old gray ball he has ever found. Since I have also seen him scrounging for used tees and spare change that may have fallen out of players' pockets, he is undoubtedly the most parsimonious of us, and he had no intention of losing a new ball in even a mud puddle.

Golf is either a very serious game, or it is a conversational sport. We Duffers tend to let anyone who crowds us play right on through, sometimes just so we can finish a discussion about education or politics (Sheldon excels in that area) or what we hope to see on the salad bar at suppertime...perhaps take a third restroom break for the round.

I have no idea whom to credit—maybe, Bob Hope—but I heard it's been said, "If you think golf is relaxing, you're not playing it right." But for us, it is relaxing; we have no intention of subscribing to golf magazines, don't spend breathless hours in front of the Golf Channel, and feel little shame if we show up in old shoes or a polo shirt that has seen its better days. We know the rules, and play by them, but we don't call out the hounds if we happen to slice a new ball into the woods either.

As custom would have it, we played our first day this year in fairly nice weather, but we knew by evening, as we sat in our favorite German restaurant, a bit tired and ready for a shower, that rain was not only in the forecast for the next morning, it was absolutely assured.

Last year, we thought we were playing in the Greater Monsoon Open, as much as it poured on us, so we headed to our favorite course early Saturday morning knowing we'd probably have to grab a rain check and head for home, which made us all a little sad because we'd be going back before we needed to stop for lunch at another favorite restaurant.

For just the briefest moment, we insanely considered playing; it was, after all, a very light rain, and the course was wide open. But the radar was lit up like a Christmas tree, so we decided that discretion is the better part of remaining dry. As we drove north and made plans for a fall trip along the way, it rained so hard I considered pulling off the road.

My friends are good men; they are fun to be with, and it would be that way whether we played golf or checkers. There is an old hat friendliness to them, and I enjoy knowing that these two predictable days each spring mean a good time for us, even if it does rain.

We like things to stay the same, I guess, and that's why we didn't mind at all when Sam fell asleep on the way home, too.

History Professor's Lessons a Study in Living

May 23, 2016

Bob Clouse had a profound and lasting effect on the people who knew him. He was a good man, a kind and compassionate one, and his full life included careers as teacher, writer, researcher, and pastor. He died on May 8 at 85.

I got to know Dr. Robert Clouse in an Indiana State University classroom. The years are beginning to run together for me now, so I'm not sure whether I had him for two history courses or three, but I do remember, above all else, the time I spent as a graduate student in his summer honors seminar on the "Age of Reason," the Enlightenment. It was, I believe, 1981.

Despite its rather imposing topic, the class proved great fun for a roomful of history nerds like us. The 15 or so students who met in old Stalker Hall—all struggling mightily to earn master's degrees while juggling full plates of work and babies and bills—liked the subject well enough, but, most of all, we loved Clouse and his disheveled, wonderfully warm demeanor.

Each day, he'd lecture a while—his digressions were wonderful—then sit in a creaking wooden student desk in the front row of the classroom while we took turns sharing our work or watching a film.

On a few occasions, we heard his soft snoring and knew that he'd fallen asleep, a thoroughly forgivable foible that we attributed to the hours he was spending in the researching and writing of countless articles and books. His passion, by the way, was "eschatology," a study of the "end times."

But none of us knew—and I'm not sure he did then, either—that Dr. Clouse's heart was failing, that in just a few years he'd receive a new one in a procedure that was far from routine in those days. He wasn't merely tired; he was exhausted. Yet, in typical Clouse fashion, he told us with a grin that he needed to either get to bed earlier or start hanging around with more entertaining people.

I remember that he was very excited to hear that I had chosen Voltaire, the French "philosophe," who was hardly a friend of the Church, as the topic for the research paper that was to be our final project. "I'm looking forward," he said with that lop-sided grin of his, "to seeing what you come up with." He meant it, too.

One of his other most endearing traits came as we made our presentations in class. Each time a student mentioned a book he or she was reading in research, Clouse would recite something specifically from its pages, often referring to other books on the topic that we might want to look into. "It's in paperback now," he'd add about the book as we laughed, for we knew that familiar line was coming. The course ended with an invitation for us to come to his home, where he and his wife, Bonnidel, could "thank us" for our hard work. I think we all went to the party, and at some point we produced a T-shirt for him, "It's in paperback now," printed across the front.

Years later, long after I had started teaching and coaching, and Bob Clouse had re-started his life with a new heart, I was back on campus one summer day. My daughter, Ellen, about 8 then, was with me, and we walked through a mostly empty Stalker Hall so I could show her where I had taken many of my classes. As we wandered by his open office door, I spied him sitting at his impossibly messy desk, his hand holding a stubborn book open so he could write down a passage from it on a notepad.

I stuck my head inside to say hello, and his face lit up, just as I remembered it always had. He asked me to step in, and when Ellen popped through the doorway, too, I could tell that it made him happy to see her; it didn't matter that they'd never met.

We chatted a while, catching up on each other's lives, but as Ellen and I fixed to leave, Clouse told me that he wanted to give her something. "I've got something here she can have," he said, as he glanced across his crammed shelves and desk. I told him he didn't need to give Ellen a gift, but by then he was already rummaging through a small closet like Fibber McGee, his words reduced to mumbles as he picked through boxes and shelves, all the while adjusting his thick-lensed glasses in the semi-darkness.

A few moments later, Clouse turned to us with a small red figurine of Buddha in his hand, telling me, as he handed it to my little girl, that one of the tenets of Buddhism is that of sharing or giving without expecting anything in return. It pleased him to give it to her.

And that is what I remember most about Robert Clouse. He was a man who gave to us, shared with us his gifts of knowledge, humor, and friendship, and the sheer joy he felt of living each day. Of those things, he had enough to fill two hearts.

The Rays of Ravishing Light and Glory
July 4, 2016

In a now famous letter sent to his wife on the eve of what would become America's first celebration of independence in 1776, John Adams wrote that he was "…apt to believe that it will be celebrated, by succeeding Generations, as the great anniversary Festival. It ought to be commemorated, as the Day of Deliverance by solemn Acts of Devotion to God Almighty."

But Adams was not suggesting that his fellow former British colonists designate the recognition of their first Independence Day by thanking their creator only. He went on to say, "It ought to be solemnized with Pomp and Parade, with Shows, Games, Sports, Guns, Bells, Bonfires and Illuminations from one End of this Continent to the other from this Time forward forever more."

Americans may be lacking at times in their thankfulness for living in a country such as ours, but we certainly have taken Adams' second recommendation to heart, for July 4th and its fireworks and parades are among the most anticipated events of our hot humid summer months.

When my children were small, they begged us to celebrate, not only by taking them to local fireworks shows—they didn't have to beg much for that—but also for buying fireworks we could set off at home. Since funds were always a consideration, we usually relented in a very limited way, but the kids enjoyed their sparklers and smoking black snakes—which did virtually nothing when lit but curl into harmless bits of crusty ash—and were delighted when I also produced a few bottle rockets and roman candles, as well.

I recall that on more than one occasion, we had to wait for a decent rain to have our personal show, for I didn't want to be known as the man who had set his own woods on fire. In a few other years, rain postponed our shows for days, but either way, we celebrated conservatively, usually while swatting mosquitoes. I never did get into firecrackers or driving across state lines to buy things that were illegal at home; I didn't, after all, want to also be known as the man who blew his own thumbs off for the sake of having a little fun.

Our Fourth of Julys have become even more tamed affairs in recent years, a mini-family reunion of sorts, since much of my wife's family—a pretty impressive number of babies included—now congregate at a local fireworks show to sit and talk and wait for nightfall. We take our lawn chairs and blankets and spread out under the stars to watch the skies light up with color, and the air thickens with that familiar acrid smoke we only sniff once a year. I can recall a half-century of such evenings, and I can't remember a single 4th where I haven't noted the "oohs and ahs" of children and adults, alike. For me, blues and greens are the colors I most enjoy.

When I was young, my parents rarely missed the chance to take us to Reeder Park in the small Wabash

River town of Montezuma, where the local fire department put on a magnificent show, and still does in the north end of town at Aztec Park. We always sat on the hillside that overlooked the park and the river, my dad off gabbing with his construction work buddies, and my mom, ever vigilant, keeping her eyes on us. We did very few things together as a family, but watching fireworks was a tradition, and I continued to follow it with my own children, that is until we initiated our new one. I recall that many folks in those days sat in the backs of their pick-up trucks, others stretching out on the hoods of their cars. There was a communal, drive-in movie sort of feel to fireworks shows then, and I still get that sense even now.

By all indication, Americans love fireworks. Records kept by the American Pyrotechnics Association tell us that last summer, alone, 285.3 million pounds of fireworks were sold in this country, over 260 million pounds of them sold locally to consumers. That impressive last figure might also account for the 12,000 or so non-fatal injuries sustained by Americans in fireworks-related accidents in 2015.

But Americans have an aptitude for hurting themselves, particularly in the summer, because over 16,000 of us sustained injuries using gas and charcoal grills last year, too.

Of course, as a teacher of history, I find stories about Adams, and his old political adversary, Thomas Jefferson, interesting as we celebrate this day. Both men may have had the same hopes in mind for the

American people, but they clearly had different ideas about and interpretations of how governments should work. In time, they became bitter political enemies and founders of America's political parties, yet after Jefferson's second term as President ended, both men reached out to reconnect with one another. They corresponded until nearly the very last day of their lives—July 4, 1826—which ironically was the 50th anniversary of their signing the Declaration of Independence.

Adams and Jefferson renewed their friendship despite their political differences, and that, too, should be their great lesson for us, because we do seem to be a divided people right now. It is said that Adams' last words were, "Jefferson survives." He couldn't have known that his old friend had died five hours before at Monticello.

In that letter to Abigail, Adams also added this: "You will think me transported with Enthusiasm but I am not. I am well aware of the Toil and Blood and Treasure, that it will cost Us to maintain this Declaration, and support and defend these States. Yet through all the Gloom I can see the Rays of ravishing Light and Glory. I can see that the End is more than worth all the Means."

I hope we all think of that sentiment as we watch our Independence Day fireworks.

Just How Fast Can 42 Years Go By?

July 18, 2016

I went to my high school reunion last month and had a great time, but I wondered at first if I had driven to the right place. When I walked through the door I saw an awful lot of old people there, then realized that I was one of them.

Of course, I recognized many of my friends from the North Vigo Class of 1974 nearly right away, although in several cases it did take some detective skills. The passing of time, a few extra pounds, or a little less hair can really change a person, so I caught myself more than once surreptitiously searching for name tags. Considering all the chests I stared at, it's a wonder I made it through the night without having my face slapped.

The last time I went to a class reunion was nearly 20 years ago; my children were still living at home in those days (my daughter was a skinny eighth grader and my son sported a flat top and played with Legos), and the conversations on that night had nothing to do with impending retirements or artificial knee replacements or how tiring it can be to take the grandkids to one of those dreadful amusement parks. But time has a way of changing things; a wild night for most of us now involves staying awake through the 11 o'clock news.

I think most of my classmates still remembered our teachers' names 20 years ago, might have even been able to recall their locker number or where they sat in

Senior English, and there were a few more of us alive then too. The last two decades have been unkind to my class in that regard, because too many of us that should have been around for our 42nd weren't.

I promised Joanie that I wouldn't make her stay too long in a crowded room of mostly strangers; she had, after all, been a trooper the night before when many of us met to gab, and a "few minutes" had stretched into two hours. I was asked to speak for a while on reunion night, so I promised her that when that was finished and I'd shaken a few hands and slapped a few backs, we'd leave. She knew that I couldn't walk away that quickly though, and said she was just fine listening to the music the DJ was playing. Hearing Don McLean and the Moody Blues took her back to her own high school years anyway; she wanted me to take my time and enjoy myself.

I graduated with well over 600 other students, starting school with some of them as far back as Nellie Neal's first grade classroom at Otter Creek Elementary. I didn't get to know a few of my closest buddies until we were in junior high school for they had started out at such exotic locales as Terre Town and Lost Creek.

Of course, I had never seen most of my classmates until we walked through North's brand new doors in 1971. We were the first class to have never attended Garfield or Gerstmeyer and were somewhat of a big-school social experiment in the making. We never knew what it was like to enjoy our lunch hours at local drug store soda fountains or cafes, and never walked the creaking floorboards or saw the ivied walls of venerable older schools either. Everything at North—except our teachers—was new.

The Class of 1974 was really a class of stars. Some of my friends played key roles on many fine athletic teams (winning the state championship in baseball our senior year and the state cross country title the year before that), and the class boasted more than its fair share of brains and beauty too. A few of my classmates went to Ivy League schools, and many others profited from very successful businesses and professional lives. But—and perhaps this is most important—my class also produced a much larger number of just plain decent, hard-working people: roofers and teachers; pharmacists and housewives; insurance agents and mechanics. Most, I believe, became responsible spouses and parents and grandparents, as well. I know I saw an awful lot of pictures of grandchildren on reunion night; one of my pals is now a great-grandfather.

When our class president, Monte McDonald, introduced me to speak, I have to admit that despite having a little experience with a microphone, I was nervous, and I must have looked it; my hands were shaking enough that I decided to read my reminiscences as they sat on a table top—the distance made me very happy that I'm not yet in need of reading glasses.

We celebrated this reunion because most of us geriatric grads are already, or soon will be, 60 years old.

Yet, there I was, in front of the class, feeling as if I were about 16 again, sweat beading on my forehead as I heard the measured voice of Wanda Williams, our high school speech teacher, saying, "You can start any time, Mr. Lunsford."

I wasn't a poor student—wasn't voted "Most Likely to Be Incarcerated," or anything like that—but I certainly was no stand-out in the classroom either. So on that night I may have been a bit moist under the arms and a tad dry of mouth when I walked to the front of the room, but I can tell you that I was proud to be from the Class of 1974. Collectively, we came from a time when it was still easy to find a payphone, when having a glass-pack muffler or an eight-track tape player in your car meant living large; a time when double-knit polyester pants and pocket combs and iron-straightened hair were in style. Gas cost us 55 cents a gallon, and I still remember sitting through *Blazing Saddles* twice, but heard Richard Nixon deny he was part of a scandal more times than that.

It was good to see so many of my old classmates again, some who were as surprised as I was when we realized how close we still live to one another. But they might as well have resided on the dark side of the moon these past years, for unless, by chance, I pass them in a grocery store or glance across a gas pump island to spot a familiar face, I rarely see these friends in the world I know now.

Of course, I probably just don't recognize some of them anymore. Sure makes a case for wearing name tags.

Finding the Man Who Died at Courcelette

August 1, 2016

In the dim light of a chaotic world, it's easy to see why so little is said these days about the Battle of the Somme, fought a hundred years ago in northern France. After great monuments had been erected to its remembrance, it seemed as though such an epic conflict, and its dead, could never be forgotten, but they nearly have been.

Even less is remembered about a solitary German artillery shell that exploded at the intersection of Candy and Sugar Trenches, not far from the small French village of Courcelette on Sept. 30, 1916, nor the two lieutenants of the Canadian Expeditionary Force—who were killed by it; after all, more than 300,000 soldiers of Britain and the Commonwealth died at the Somme. But the family of one of those men—Fred Foley of the 26th Infantry Battalion, Second Division of the Canadian Expeditionary Force hasn't allowed his memory to fade.

The titanic struggle of the Somme, fought along a 15-mile front, was actually an entire offensive. Beginning in July, and lasting until November, it was to be the decisive battle of the Great War. But despite great Allied optimism with their plan of attack, the war grimly carried on for two more years.

Over a million men in the British, French, and German armies were killed or wounded at the

Somme—the British fired off nearly 2 million artillery shells in the week before it even began—yet only about six miles of ground was exchanged between the two great forces that met there. In the end, the battle came to symbolize the frustration, waste, and senselessness of World War I.

Foley's grandnephew, Joshua Powers, hasn't forgotten what happened at Courcelette; in fact, he took it upon himself to ensure that his great uncle's memory be kept alive. The wooden cross that was placed on the spot where Fred and fellow lieutenant, Ernie Welch, were killed was eventually obliterated by shell fire, but thanks to modern technology and a great deal of determination, Powers has stood at the exact place, the culminating experience of a trip he organized for himself and eight other members of his family.

"I have always had an interest in military history," Powers says. "My grandmother and great aunt occasionally spoke about Fred in a wistful way. The cottage in Saint John [New Brunswick] that my great aunt owned had some pictures of him, and that is where the seeds got planted. What really cemented it was my aunt's [his mother's sister] scanning Fred's letters and sharing them with all of us. Finally, I have always been fascinated by the Somme's tragic place in British history and knew the 100th anniversary would be a memorable and fitting time to go."

A professor of educational leadership and Associate Vice-President for Academic Affairs at Indiana State University, Powers saw to it that he and his family made the pilgrimage to the fields of Flanders and the Somme battlefield from June 29 to July 2. His and their recollections of what they saw and felt there are available at sommepilgrimage.wordpress.com, a blogsite on which they continue to add impressions. Along with Powers and his mother, Marcia Dunning, the group included his daughters Casey and Katlyn, son Koby, wife Susan, niece Caroline, father-in-law Bob Metzler, and sister Lucia Matule, and her husband, Matt, (who live in Amsterdam, Netherlands).

Foley was the son of a Saint John potter, just 22 years old when he departed for England exactly one year before his death. He had finished a single term at the University of New Brunswick and wanted to be a civil engineer. Arriving on the French coast on July 1, it is possible that he heard the explosions of the British mines that opened the offensive; he lived 90 days at the front, which was about two months longer than the average British officer's life expectancy in battle. His body, like those of nearly half of the dead of the Great War, was never recovered.

Using GPS links to official trench locations and death records, Powers was able to steer his family to the exact spot where his great uncle died, now in a French farm field.

When asked what it was like knowing that he stood at the place his great uncle had died a century before, Powers said, "First, was satisfaction at having 'found' a missing soldier. The records clearly indicate he's at that spot. But, having 'found' him, does that mean he's not really among the thousands of missing now? Did I somehow lessen that incredible honor and ultimate sacrifice associated with the 'unknown soldier'?"

"My great grandmother and grandfather, and the family, received only a telegram in early October that Fred had been killed. No smartly dressed officers arrived at their door equipped to handle the inevitable grief to come. Months went by until they received a letter from an officer dug out alive from the bunker (Lt. James Cecil Stuart) who could relay more details. Other families didn't even get this, just a kind, and mass produced, certificate of appreciation from the King of England," Powers added.

Powers poignantly sprinkled soil brought from Foley's New Brunswick home on the unmarked grave. "I was powerfully moved by the contrast in colors of soil between France and Canada. It was starting to rain, and I could see it already working down, on its way to Fred. That may sound like a cliché, but it is what I thought, and there was a certain closure or full circle aspect to it," he said.

In 1936, Fred's sister, Violet, traveled to France to witness the unveiling of the monument at Vimy, engraved with the names of 11, 285 unknown dead of the Canadian Expeditionary Force in France, including Fred Foley; King Edward VIII was present for its unveiling. On that day, "Vi" wore a beret in honor of her brother; it bore the insignia of the 26th Canadian Battalion; Powers replicated the hats for his group to wear.

Among the many tributes at Vimy, Vi, who lived an incredible life herself—dying at age 106—heard Reverend Cecil Owen speak in remembrance. Among his comments was this: "We must educate our children in the finer aspects of courage and sacrifice which emerged during the war so that they will remember the heroism and deeper lessons which should have resulted from it."

The kind of world we are seeing now would perhaps disappoint Fred Foley and the millions who fought and died in the Great War, for it was called the "war to end all wars."

What America Needs Is a $50 Freezer

August 28, 2016

Our upright freezer died last week. It wasn't that old—we had it about 14 years—but it has apparently frozen its last store-bought pizza and pot pie. One minute the thing was working fine in our garage, and the next it went into a rapid decline, its digital temperature read-out rising hour by hour like a critical heart rate. It will be missed, particularly because both my wife and I hoped it would run long enough for one of our children to use someday.

I know our expectation for its long life may have been unrealistic in these days of built-in obsolescence, but both sets of our parents had freezers—chest types—that lasted over half-a-century, so we expected ours to make it to a more graceful retirement too. As anyone who has had to do it will tell you, trying to clean out a dripping freezer is not one of life's finer moments.

Our first freezer was already well-used by the time we bought it out of someone else's garage; I think I paid $30 for it. I remember bringing it home and rubbing a few rusty spots with sand paper, then touching it up with a can of spray paint. It lasted for years, but when it finally proved inadequate for our growing family, we bought our upright, proudly stocking it with frozen veggies, cookie dough, and the raspberries my wife picked along our fence rows.

As I write this, we await a repairman, expecting the worst, because to tell you the truth, I am unimpressed with how our unit is put together. Being both a fix-it type (as long as the job can be done with a screwdriver and a pair of pliers) and cheap, I pulled the freezer away from the wall as we heard its earliest wheezes. I scrubbed its copper coils and vacuumed its spider webs and accumulated lint and dirt, and inspected for leaks. I thought I'd find a full drain pan, but instead found only a few dessicated beetles that had unwittingly crawled into what would become their own mausoleum. Other than an annoying hum, I couldn't find anything obviously wrong.

Despite it being a "major" brand, I discovered that our freezer looks as if it was built out of old Japanese transistor radio parts. Its flimsy guts make me wonder how it lasted as long as it did, for its compressor is about the size of a cantaloupe and its fan motor is no bigger than those I've seen in old erector sets.

Unlike ours, the freezer I grew up with was a behemoth, a huge old round-shouldered Philco that had to have weighed a ton and may have been built with surplus World War II tank armor. My mom bought it used for $50 in 1951 and it sat in our utility room forever. It was still in our house—and running—when the place was sold over four decades later.

I can remember a repairman being called a time or two over the years for my parents' machine, but otherwise that old thing just kept on rattling and blowing warm air for as long as I can remember, literally. Things were expected to last in those days, and usually did.

I also recall the countless hours I spent as a kid napping and playing on the floor near it, for its warm gusts and steady hum were pleasant on a cold day; our friendly gray cat, Tom, often joined me there for an afternoon snooze or storybook session. Our new freezer has no such romance attached to it: it merely occupies a corner, not far from the water heater and recycling cans.

I seriously doubt that my mom got a manual with hers, but if she did, I'm certain that it, too, was superior to the one I have for our freezer. I am a diagram man, so I thumbed through ours in search of a parts list and a schematic so I could see a few likely suspects of the trouble.

Instead, our flimsy manual takes great pains to discuss "How to set the temperature control," then abruptly changes over to read in French. There is no parts list, no diagram of the machine's innards either. Instead there was a worthless list of "troubleshooting" tips. "Be sure your freezer is plugged in to a receptacle," it reads. Do I really need to be reminded of that?

With all of our frozen food now turning to stone in someone else's freezer, our attention focuses on whether we get this one fixed or just buy another. If we go the second route, we'll consider just about any brand, listen to the recommendations of friends, and do some reading before we buy.

But I think I'll call the people who bought my parents' place too. They may give me a good deal on the old Philco.

Celebrating the Gifts of Being 60

September 12, 2016

If all goes well, and I wake up tomorrow morning, I will be 60 years old. It is an age that I once thought unimaginable.

I have tried to put my birthday into some sort of perspective these past few weeks as I've approached the big day, and most of my thoughts can be summed up pretty well with a simple question: "How did I get this far so fast?" I used to think 60-year-olds were ancient, fossils, 'older than dirt,' as they say. I don't feel that way anymore.

Reaching 60 isn't the accomplishment it was just a few decades ago when now-curable diseases ran rampant and more people literally worked themselves into early graves. Our perception of being 60 has decidedly changed in recent years too, and that, despite its costs, has to be credited to our doctors and scientists and labor unions, and probably the prayers of our mothers.

When I was a boy, I thought 60-year-old people were very old, and they contributed mightily to that notion themselves. My grandfather would have never dreamed of being seen in a pair of shorts or wearing a pair of comfortable running shoes; his clothes were always practical and dull and well-used. Now, more grandpas are running mini-marathons and getting hair plugs and driving rebuilt muscle cars. Although we may be creeping toward a national immaturity crisis in the near future, I like the trend that more of us "senior citizens" feel better about our age and want to be more active. I know I don't plan to spend the next 20 years in a recliner with a remote control in my hands, that is, unless *Gunsmoke* reruns are on.

I don't believe I ever saw my grandmother, who died at 60, in a pair of pants, except at berry-picking time, and still nearly worshiping her memory, I most often associate her with her sewing and canning and housedresses and black and white television and a party telephone line. She would have considered it ridiculous that a woman her age be seen riding a bike; there was mending and cooking to do. By the way, I think more households could use a return to the self-sufficiency she practiced, but I don't think there's anything wrong with grandmas using "Facetime" to visit with their grandkids either.

We aren't planning any special celebration on my 60th; perhaps a nice dinner with the family. Joanie, who has already hit the milestone, wanted no festivities, no fete, when she turned 60, and I'd like mine to be an understated affair too.

I know I am getting older, because, besides a few books, I can't think of a single thing I'd like to have for my birthday. It's frightening, but T-shirts or socks seem alright as gifts now. If the pattern I've seen established by my father-in-law and dad and grandfather holds true, many of those kinds of things will probably be found in the back of my closet someday when my kids are cleaning out my belongings. They'll be unopened because I wanted to keep them for "good," then forgot I had them.

Although I hope to have a long life—like that of my great-uncle, Tom, who went past 90—I know I made it much, much longer than my mom's dad, whom I never met. He passed at 38 and spent the majority of his too-short life working in a coal mine. I do think that at 60 a man has had enough longevity to look back at life and reflect a little; Grandpa John Hill never got that chance.

Truly, I have had a wonderful life—yes, a bit like George Bailey. I've made no Trumpian fortune (remember, I teach school in a small, rural community), and I think I can now rule out still having a shot at a Pulitzer Prize, but I've enjoyed years with a wonderful wife and family and have had great health, and it looks like I'll be able to retire without having to worry about wolves scratching at my door.

I have never been without a job, although there have been times of much griping about it. I can't say that there was anything I would have rather spent my life doing than teaching, and I sure wish legislators and politicians would just let teachers teach kids; there is a time coming when no one will want to teach anymore. Actually, we're just about to that point now.

I still have most of my hair, and I hope I don't say that too vainly, but I don't have to invest much in hats. I'm okay with that because I don't much like to wear a hat. I also have a nice home that is warm in the winter and cool in the summer; I have water and food in my refrigerator, and clothes on my back. I have more shoes and tools than I will ever need too. In short, I am better off than most people, and that is just one reason that I am happier than just about everyone I know. I have good friends too; the kind that would come over and help me work on a septic tank or a hot roof; the kind I can spend a few hours fishing with.

Yes, I sure have changed my idea of what old is. When I was still in my teens, my cousin, Roger, was in his mid-20s, and he abruptly got married and gave his baseball card collection to me, then moved away. I thought he was getting "old" because of that.

Wait a minute; I think I've already told that story before in another column. I'm told 60-year-olds do that sort of thing…

I hope I can keep a decent sense of humor as the years go by; most folks who are older than I am say it is going to be a basic necessity. I will have to learn to embrace the fact that I am going to lose my car keys more often, and won't be able to do some of the things I used to do, like jump and hit off the back tees, or ride amusement park rides that go in circles.

As a matter of fact, I was reminded of the sense of humor thing just yesterday. I decided it was time I cleaned a few combs I have been using, and after giving them a good soaking, I grabbed an old tooth brush we keep under the bathroom sink for scrubbing tight spots in the shower and around the faucets. I worked the combs over pretty well and set them aside just as I remembered I also needed to brush my teeth.

Well, I think you know where I'm going with this. "I don't use a glittery purple toothbrush I thought," as I was in mid-sweep along my molars. And that's when I saw my yellow brush sitting in a cup two feet away.

The whole incident reminded me of one other thing I've learned in 60 years: You should always have a good rinse after you brush.

On Why We Aren't Moving to Florida

October 10, 2016

My son and his wife took a long trip a few weeks ago, and of course, Joanie and I took a shift at watching our grandson, Daniel. We looked forward to his coming to the house for a few days, for although we have served as babysitters, we had never had him over for an extended stay.

Daniel will have had his first birthday by the time this story runs, which means he's now at the age where crawling is passé and walking is no longer a consideration: he runs everywhere, and the bruises on his head and the scrapes on his arms and knees are visible proof that he's no expert at it yet; he has become a speed-walking "Band-Aid" commercial.

The trip proved to be an adjustment for the parents as well. Daughter-in-law Lucy wrote what amounted to an *Encyclopedia Britannica* of instructions for those who shared in the duties: medication dosages; bed and meal times; Daniel's likes and dislikes. We assured her that we had some experience in the care of children, and although we may do some things differently, Daniel would be fine.

Just a few minutes with Daniel had us recalling what a physical challenge it can be to keep up with a 1-year-old; the contestants on *American Gladiator* don't have workouts that approach watching that boy. He's big for his age, so carrying him very far is like holding a squirming bag of concrete mix, and feeding him—I still have flashbacks about "pelican" bibs and pureed peas—can actually be a little nauseating. We weren't always in the vicinity of a bathtub at mealtimes, so I considered loading a portable power washer in our van for whenever we took him somewhere. After all, it isn't easy raking macaroni and cheese and mashed potatoes out of a kid's hair.

One of the biggest concerns we had before Daniel's visit was that we hadn't had a toddler stay in our house for a long time. We no longer had electrical outlet plug covers in place, nor had our kitchen cabinets locked shut. My desk alone held a dizzying array of items a little guy could wreak havoc with: pocket knives and keys and paperweights. I have a roll-top desk that is rarely shut, but that policy changed within the first 10 minutes we had him.

We hadn't thought that the oak plant stand in our living room would become one of Daniel's prime targets. Or should I say, obsession? He was bound and determined from the first time he saw it that he was going to pull it over and inspect what was sitting on it. We eventually had to move it into another room and shut the door. In fact, we soon had our bedroom filled with other things his grabbing little paws were after; it looked like we were having a garage sale in there.

We hadn't considered the fact that our two house cats—Edgar and Jack—were not used to having a boy in the house either. They are accustomed to a rather sedate existence, a quiet and orderly house, a welcoming lap or pat on the head, and food bowls always in the same place. It didn't take long for Daniel to introduce himself to Edgar's tail, and as for Jack, I don't think I saw him until after Daniel was hauled off to bed each night. Joanie and I suspected that Daniel may have dined on a little cat food before we moved the dishes.

We had forgotten what it was like to take a little

guy like Daniel on the road, too. When he was first brought over, we inherited a pile of bags and sacks and satchels that suggested the Joads had arrived in California. Much of that stash had to go with us when we took him places. His stroller, which cost more than a Land Rover (that thing has pneumatic tires and cup holders), had to go, as did, of course, his new baby seat, his diaper bag, his snacks... I really came to appreciate what mothers do on a daily basis, because I discovered that I could carry Daniel, or I could handle his accessories, but packing both around required an Andean llama.

We did make his time with us a bit of a road show. We took him to his very first football game, which he completely ignored in favor of running on the school's all-weather track (we were impressed that the little dude stayed inside his lane all night). That evening never really cooled off, and it featured a wilting humidity that had us both soaked in sweat. I was about as fresh as an old dishrag by halftime, but Daniel still seemed to have plenty of gas left in his tank.

The next day we hauled him to an auction. It was yet another hot late September day, but he took it like a champ, or I should say Joanie did. While I bid on a number of items (one of which I'll have to write about later), Joanie kept Daniel occupied, logging miles on his stroller and stuffing him with a pre-lunch snack, then lunch, then an after-lunch snack, then his after-lunch snack snack. After a quick snooze on the trip home, he was awake and raring to go just after I carried him through our door. I think I heard him mutter his first real words: "Hey, where's the plant stand you moved?"

We also took Daniel to church the next morning, which amounted to us walking in late for a tag-team wrestling match. He later went to a baby shower with Joanie, toward which I am sure that someday, like any full-blooded American male, he will develop a deep aversion. But since there were other children there, he was happy to stay a while, smashing cake into his scalp while being handed off like a football from grandmother to aunt to cousin.

On the night Evan and Lucy came home—some nine days after leaving on their trip—we took Daniel over to their house and gave him his bath and let him play well past his bedtime. Several times, we tried to get him to bed down, but it was if he knew his mom and dad were coming home, so we finally decided to let him stay up. Of course, no less than 10 minutes before they pulled in the drive, he was sound asleep, too exhausted to go on. I know we were just as tired as he was.

Dave Barry once wrote that "…the best baby-sitters, of course, are the grandparents. You feel completely comfortable entrusting your baby to them for long periods, which is why most of them flee to Florida."

We don't want to move to Florida at all. But I think we're going have to leave the plant stand in the bedroom for a while.

Go Ahead: Hold Your Nose and Vote

November 7, 2016

As my American History class begins each year, I take great pains to convince students that the subject is worthy of their attention. It is a hard sell these days. One lesson I use is called, "The More Things Change, The More They Stay the Same." The title, an age-old adage, is most apt in this election year.

This year, along with photographs of Donald Trump and Hillary Clinton, I showed the students a statement by "political insider" J. Sterling Morton, who said, "I am going to shut my eyes, hold my nose, vote, and then go home and disinfect myself." After the kind of political year we've all endured, his is a sentiment to which many of us can relate.

With the appearance of the pictures, some of my kids snickered and shook their heads, the words of parents and grandparents, television news commentators and opinionated friends, ringing in their heads. It is only after I revealed that Morton was speaking of the election of 1896 and candidates Republican William McKinley and Democrat William Jennings Bryan that I saw a few students have "get it" moments.

I tend to look at today's news through yesterday's eyeglasses. What has happened, has, for the most part, happened before. If there is a grim national dissatisfaction with this election, it is nothing new. We need to pay attention to our own history; there have been Donalds and Hillarys before. Despite its nasty rhetoric, its low blows, and its name-calling, tomorrow's election is not unique.

Americans have both endured and promoted dirty politics since our nation's inception, and many of our Founders—including Thomas Jefferson and John Adams—were not immune to taking the occasional cheap shot themselves.

Had they and their supporters had access to around-the-clock news coverage and Twitter and Madison Avenue advertising, I am convinced that nearly all Americans of that era would be as nauseated, as sated, as thoroughly disgusted, and exhausted as we are today.

After voting early last week, a friend of mine said that she felt "depressed and dirty." She added that not long after receiving the polling place sticker that reads, "I Voted," she wasn't proud to wear it: "I actually feel like voting this time is a violation, an assault against me," she added.

Amid allegations of fraud and email scandals, groping and misogyny, it is important to remember that in the election of 1860, Abraham Lincoln's campaign managers mocked political opponent Stephen Douglas's height (he was, to put it mildly, "vertically challenged"), while Douglas supporters in turn referred to Lincoln as, "the leanest, lankest, most ungainly mass of legs and arms and hatchet face ever strung on a human frame." One anti-Abe newspaper said that Lincoln was "a horrid looking wretch . . . sooty and scoundrelly in aspect. . ."

Criticism toward Hillary's Bill and Donald's Melania is nothing new either. For instance, the election of 1828— which might boast the nastiest rhetoric ever—saw National Republican John Quincy Adams' campaign accuse Democrat Andrew Jackson's wife, Rachel, of adultery since the old "Hero of New Orleans" had courted her before she had officially divorced; she was often called an "American Jezebel," he a "murderer," as a result of his dueling days. On the other hand, Jackson's people accused JQA of flesh-peddling at least one American woman to the Russian czar when Adams served as the American Ambassador to Russia, and said that Adams' wife, Louisa, who had not been born in the United States, could not be trusted.

These are not isolated examples: Democrats tried to smear Rutherford B. Hayes in the 1876 campaign by claiming he had drunkenly shot his own mother, and had even stolen the pay of dead soldiers under his command during the Civil War. In 1844, Whigs claimed that they had proven—through the use of a book that did not exist—that James K. Polk had been a slave-trader. A story in a Federalist newspaper asked readers that if Jefferson were to be elected in 1800, "Are you prepared to see your dwellings in flames, female chastity violated, and children writhing on the pike?" In 1856, opponents of James Buchanan, who suffered from a congenital neck condition that caused him to tilt his head, claimed the disorder was the result of a failed attempt to hang himself.

And, one can see why Morton was pretty

disgusted with both McKinley and Bryan—both campaigns were cranking out prodigious amounts of propaganda. For instance, McKinley's friends had influence in an anonymous article that appeared in the "New York Times" under the headline, "Is Bryan Crazy?" It suggested that psychiatric experts believed Bryan suffered from "megalomania, delusions of grandeur and quarrulent logorrhea (I had to look that one up)." One consultant was quoted as saying of Bryan, "I should like to examine him as a degenerate."

I'm going to my polling place tomorrow morning and will cast my ballot. I don't want a pat on the back, won't need a sticker, and can't stand to think about hearing the gloating of "We won," the moaning of "It's rigged," and the endless television analysis that is bound to come afterward.

On Wednesday morning, after the smoke has cleared, we will have a new president-elect. I hope that whether it be Donald Trump or Hillary Clinton that he or she will be gracious in either victory or defeat, and that in January we will have a peaceful transition of power.

I believe that we are better than this year's election, but history shows us that sometimes, we are not.

The Case of the Wandering Wedding Ring

November 21, 2016

My wife's wedding ring went missing last week. She was, of course, upset about it because she swore she remembered putting all three of her rings—an engagement band, an anniversary ring I gave her a few years ago, and her wedding ring—in the same place she does every night before she takes her shower and plods off to bed. It was gone the next morning.

As is most often the case in such a crisis, Joanie discovered the ring's absence just a few minutes before we had to leave the house in the morning, not for work, but for an appointment in Indianapolis. She knew she'd stew all day if she didn't find the ring, and I could see, even after I pushed my cereal aside to join in the search, her increasing frustration as she ransacked our house in desperation.

Had I been Perry Mason, the hard-boiled attorney turned detective that I used to watch in reruns in my grandmother's living room, I'd have immediately dispatched tough guy Paul Drake to punch a few jaws, or loyal Della Street to get on the phone to fences and informants, but we were already late in leaving, so unlike Raymond Burr, I thought we had better just scram and search for the ring when we got back home.

The engagement and wedding rings were my Grandmother Daisy's before they were Joanie's. My mom gave them to me not long after her mom had passed, more than suggesting to me that I had better get them on Joanie's finger sooner rather than later. Although Joanie has loved the rings, I've always thought I'd buy her a new wedding band when I could better afford it, but I never have.

"I love my rings," she'd say, somewhat offended

when I suggested it to her, for she religiously has them cleaned and inspected for damage and wear. Despite their being over 70 years old now, I believe they have to look about as good as the day my step-grandfather bought them, at a downtown Terre Haute jeweler, I suspect.

I had a hard time pulling Joanie out of the house that morning, particularly after I found her on the bathroom floor on her hands and knees going through the trash can, that after she had already inspected every corner and crevice in our place, flashlight in hand. She wandered from room to room, her right index fingernail between her teeth, muttering things like, "I know I was there, but had it on when I went here, so it has to be..."

I've lost things that have had me mumbling too; we all have, particularly car keys. I'll never forget the time I lost a pocketknife I inherited after my dad died; I may very well have written about that black day before. It wasn't just that it was a good knife—one I had with me every single day for ten or so years by then—it was my dad's; I had seen him use it a hundred times.

I thought I had lost the knife in New Salem, Illinois, as I walked the re-created roads of the little burg where Abraham Lincoln had gotten his start in business and politics, and some say fallen in love too. But as it had turned out, it had dropped out of my pocket on the tour bus that took me the 20 miles or so out there from Springfield.

Nearly two weeks after stewing about the knife,

I had an epiphany and called the charter bus company that had taken us to New Salem. Sure enough, the driver checked the seats I thought I had been in and around, and I soon had the knife in my pocket again. In a single moment of clarity, I thought of the solution—not unlike Mason in "The Case of the Dead Ringer," perhaps. And I believed that once Joanie calmed down, maybe even lost a little sleep over it, she'd figure out what had happened too.

Two days went by, and the ring failed to appear; there had been no "Eureka Moment," no sudden revelation of, "That's where it is!" I noticed Joanie distracted, staring off into space, her brow furled, her hard-worked forefinger nail now close to a nub. She prayed over, hoped for, and looked in about every place she knew she had been the night before the ring's disappearing act, but to no avail.

I have to admit that I was stumped too. Mason would have simply applied the pressure to a disgruntled wife or straying husband, a crooked business associate or secret lover on the witness stand until they broke down and screamed (lifting themselves halfway out of the chair to do it), "I didn't mean to do it. I didn't plan to take the ring. I didn't know anybody even cared for it that much!"

Sunday morning came around, and I awoke with my skull pounding, not after a few too many whiskey and sodas, as Mason would have had after hours, but because I had a head cold. I told Joanie I'd drive to church later, but at that time all I wanted was a cup of coffee and a long shower.

Joanie had been gone a while by the time I pulled myself out of my chair to head to the bathroom for that shower, and for some reason I thought it the appropriate time to shake the rugs in my old breezeway office. Reaching down to grab one, I saw the ring lying on the carpet, neatly tucked up against a wall. It was nearly invisible. Joanie later told me the ring had apparently fallen into some laundry she was taking to our bathroom hamper, then fell off the clothes into oblivion. An hour or so later, and for the second time in our lives, I happily handed my wife that thin little band of gold and diamonds.

Despite the rather anti-climatic end to the 'Case of the Wandering Wedding Ring,' I have to admit that even Mason didn't get as good a pay-off as the one I had; I don't think I ever saw Della Street kiss him.

The Pleasures of Coffee and Crosswords

December 5, 2016

One of life's great pleasures comes for me on those rare mornings when instead of heading out the door I am planted at the kitchen table with a cup of hot coffee in one hand and a chewed ballpoint pen in the other.

The yard may need mowing or snowy sidewalks shoveled, but those, and a dozen other chores, can always wait a few minutes while I work the crossword puzzle in the newspaper.

I'm not sure when I got into the habit of tackling

the daily crossword puzzle. I have always been a word man—brought up in a household of books—but other than the "word search" I often found in my grandparents' *Modern Maturity* magazine every month or so, I can't say I had much of a passion for such pastimes. I sure have the bug now, though.

More than anyone else I've ever known, my father-in-law, Gilbert Dickey, was a crossword devotee. Some of my best memories of him come from the dozens of times I walked into his living room to see him sitting in his favorite recliner, dime store reading glasses balanced on his nose, a strand of uncombed hair across his forehead, working a crossword with a Farm Bureau ink pen. Always in work pants and shirt, he'd balance his arm on a raised crossed leg and have very little to say until his puzzle was done.

Over the years, my kids and wife must have bought Gib a hundred crossword puzzle books. But I think he liked those he found in the *Tribune-Star* or *The Daily Clintonian* best, most often folding his newspapers into quarter sections to do them. He may have had hay to bale or a tractor tire to change, but Gib always tackled that crossword as if it was all he planned to do that day; I appreciate his influence.

Crossword puzzles really haven't been around very long. Despite my belief that surely ancient Egyptians or Greeks were mulling over their early development, the first widely-published crossword, which was originally named a "Word Cross," is credited to Arthur Wynne, a game page editor of the

New York World in 1913.

The often-repeated story goes that as Wynne spent a winter afternoon trying to come up with new games for a special Christmas edition of the paper, he recalled the "word squares" his grandfather (he was originally from Liverpool) had taught him. A word square is solved when all the words read the same way both horizontally and vertically, but Wynne created a puzzle in which the "across" words were different than the "down" words, and had more words in it. His puzzle has none of the black squares we most often associate with crosswords.

The challenge of Wynne's puzzle must have appealed to those readers who wanted to solve at least one problem in their lives; many wrote to the paper in praise of it, so puzzles followed in the Sundays to come, including the week in which the men who set the games page up reversed the words in the title, accidentally creating the term, "Cross Word."

When the *World* eventually tried to drop the popular puzzles, readers were outraged, so editors, despite the difficulty of editing and setting up the puzzles, carried on. Crosswords proved so difficult to include in newspapers that no rival of the *World* wanted to print them. For nearly 10 years, it was the only newspaper in the country that carried the game.

Now, of course, I have no trouble finding crossword puzzles. Although I prefer putting pen to paper, I often turn to my computer or tablet for a change of pace, including the daily puzzle offered up by *USA Today*. Among my favorite puzzles are those with news-related items put together by the popular magazine, *The Week*. Since those take a little extra time for me to work, I have stacks of the magazines we've read ready to go for vacations and weekends. My work day gets in the way too, but it isn't uncommon for me to work a crossword at my desk at lunch or in a doctor's office waiting room.

Of course, there's conflicting evidence about whether crosswords do much more than give us a daily challenge or help us pass the time. One on-line medical journal I consulted mentioned "cognitive reserves" that aged crossword puzzle solvers develop, and suggested that one study showed those who worked crosswords held off age-related dementia 2.54 years longer than a like group that avoided word puzzles. All I can say is that I hope that is the case, and the studies that show coffee helps the brain encourage me too, for I rarely work a crossword without a cup of joe nearby.

When an English teacher-librarian marries an English teacher-writer, it is a safe bet that it is a match made in a word-related heaven; such is the case for my wife and me. Joanie is an avid "Jumble" solver, the fastest at it of anyone I can imagine. Although I too tackle those, I am more devoted to crosswords than she is.

I visited a website a few days ago that offers free crosswords and soon discovered that its "hard" puzzles are, indeed, just that. It took longer than usual for me to get through a "medium" puzzle, but as soon as I was through with it, I headed back to the more difficult level.

Besides coffee, having a little stubbornness helps when working crosswords too.

Christmas Wish Lists, Past and Present

December 19, 2016

With it being the week before Christmas, I am in my usual nostalgic mood tonight. As I write this, a heater is wafting toasty air across my feet, and a few red and green Christmas bulbs twinkle in my window. It takes but a little daydreaming to feel the warm old house in which I grew up years ago.

We didn't have Cratchit Family Christmases when I was a boy. My parents were far from wealthy, and I know we had a few winters when gift-giving had to take a stationwagon's backseat to the heating oil and grocery bills, but I can only remember my brother and sister and I having plenty to open under the Christmas tree each year, although even then I suspected my parents got precious little for themselves.

I am prompted to these thoughts by finding my 11-year-old nephew's wish list from five years ago. I had it in a folder of column ideas that I had tucked under what I thought was my only folder of ideas, all stashed together in a messy pile that takes up space on the right-hand side of my desk. I rarely throw much away.

His list, which was typed by his mom, was funny to us when we got it, so I kept it handy for a night just like tonight when none of the ideas I have in my head can make themselves into a story. The list has nearly yellowed as Carson has gone from an age of footed trapdoor pajamas to basketball jerseys and showing off for girls and eye-rolling at bad jokes. He's getting to the age now where he holds most adults at some distance, and I know he's probably tired of hearing bits of my sage advice and bad jokes.

Carson is probably much too mature now to want to play with the "Dr. Dreadful Edible Zombie Maker" he was asking for then, although since I seem to have reversed my course and am heading back to childhood with each passing year, I have to admit that I wouldn't mind spending a few hours with that myself.

He loved practical jokes even then, so along with edible zombies and a dump truck and a farm set, he wanted a new "whoopee" cushion. We already knew he had a hand buzzer, a nail-through-the-finger, and a set of fly-riddled plastic ice cubes.

Although I spent quite a bit of anxious time looking through the Sears *Wishbook* and Spiegel's catalogue when I was a kid, I don't recall ever handing my mom or grandmother a Christmas list. That's just not how Christmas worked with us.

I have no problem whatsoever with Carson having a list, but I will say that despite getting more than a few things I didn't really want when I was his age (for instance, a belt with my name embossed on it), I mostly got what I went to bed dreaming of; my mother somehow knew without my ever really telling her what I had my eye on.

I'm sure she was looking over my shoulder as I salivated over those glossy catalog pages filled with plastic cowboy and Indian sets and cap pistols, and every year, she found that special something I could spend the next 12 months wearing out, almost as much as the knees of my J.C. Penney blue jeans.

As I have described in annual Christmas columns before, our Christmas tree most often sat on an unheated and tiled front porch, and I still remember that very few Christmases went by without its leaky old windows sporting a coating of frost.

On Christmas Eve, my parents would leave the doors to the porch open to heat the room for the big morning, and they'd leave the utilitarian gas log burning under its faux logs in our brick fireplace all night. I can still smell the scent of Douglas fir in my imaginary trips through that house, and I am thankful that at Christmas I remember only good things when so many others find it a lonely and empty time.

As we age, Joanie and I have much shorter lists than those we started compiling for our first Christmases together; she's an organizer, so it is still an essential part of her being to make everyone happy.

It seems we wanted so many things then, because we truly needed them: clothes for school, a briefcase, a pair of good boots. ... I know that I quit trying to buy clothes for her; I knew she didn't want to do it, but often she'd discreetly return those kinds of things to the store, telling me they didn't fit quite right, and I understood.

Now, our lists are shorter, and in the past few years we haven't bothered to put much down at all. Instead, I keep a mental list in my head year 'round, not for me, but for my grandson. I often see things in stores that remind me of the gifts my Santa Claus mother left for me under our tree. So, I hope the telescope or plastic soldiers or *Illustrated Classics* or pocketknife I'll buy for him in the years to come make him as happy as they did me.

It may sound selfish to hope that that my boy's little boy can grow up in a world that is safer and happier than the one we've seen this year, but if he could, I'd trade every cap pistol memory I have to make that happen. But since I can't do that, we'll just have to settle for what we think he'll enjoy.

Maybe a whoopee cushion would be good.

Mashed Potatoes and a Pelican Bib, Please
April 24, 2017

Years ago, we invited a teaching friend over for a weeknight spaghetti supper. He was a young bachelor, new to the profession, unmarried, living in a tiny apartment, and in need of a good meal, so when I mentioned how good of a cook Joanie was, he eagerly took me up on the offer.

We were hardly an old married couple; our daughter wasn't quite 2, and our house, purchased the summer before, was far from being a palace. Our roof leaked and the floors creaked, and we had just spent a miserable winter battling frozen drains that had us dipping water out of the sinks every night and kicking our furnace every morning. Our window panes rattled in the wind, and we hated the orange carpet in the kitchen.

But we were grateful to have the place, proud of the changes that we were slowly making to it, and pleased that Scott would be able to sit with us at our old oak table for supper. By the time he found our driveway, we already had Ellen in her chair, a plate of spaghetti ready; she was resplendent in a "pelican bib," the plastic tray on a collar that was so popular in those days. In some ways, the thing always reminded me of a Roman foot soldier's armored breast plate, appropriate I suppose when fighting an invasion of smashed peas, slopped carrots, or tossed scrambled eggs.

Short of spreading a painting tarp out on the floor, which we had done before we bought the bib, we had come to appreciate the thing because it saved us from the tediousness of collecting what hadn't made it into Ellen's mouth from that aforementioned carpet. The rather repulsive chore of scraping out the bib's tray —never pleasant—still beat the alternatives.

Our friend had never heard of a pelican bib before, nor apparently had he been forced to watch an 18-month-old child eat spaghetti with her hands. We were in the process of teaching Ellen how to use a spoon and fork, but she usually tossed those aside, enjoying instead the more tactile pleasure of handling her food as well as eating it. Until you've had mashed potatoes between your fingers, I guess it's hard to knock it ...

Within a quarter-hour, despite the pleasant conversation, our friend had seen enough. Ellen's face and curly blonde hair, by then a glowing orange muddle of smeared pasta sauce and bread crumbs, had our dinner companion's eyes fixed intently on his own plate, a look of horror and nausea spreading across his countenance as he tried to avoid looking at her. He had not only watched Ellen as she had stuffed handfuls of spaghetti into her mouth with both hands, but he had unwisely glanced into the bib's tray to witness the disgusting mixture of dropped and partially chewed food deposited there.

"No offense," he gagged, as if he needed an airline vomit bag, "but how can you look at that every night?"

If I recall, Joanie told him, "If you think that's bad, don't look in the diaper pail, or you're a goner. That's just part of having a baby."

We have an 18-month-old grandson now, and it has become one of the highlights of our week to stop by my son's place to pick Daniel up for a day with Grandma and Grandpa. We usually push him around a home improvement store a while (he loves ceiling fans and tools), take him to a park to run off a little energy, then we head out for lunch at a local cafeteria-type restaurant for the "early bird." He nearly always wants macaroni and cheese, mashed potatoes, and green beans, but we give him a spoonful of whatever we have on our plates too.

We did just that a few days ago, and despite our best efforts, within 20 minutes Daniel's high chair tray looked like a jackal had fed on it. It was impossible to keep his place at the table presentable; I intended to leave a generous tip.

"I think we need to see if we can get him a pelican bib," I told Joanie as we considered hosing him off at a car wash.

"We'd have to sit away from everyone else. You remember the night we had Scott over for supper, don't you?"

Now that I think of it, I wonder if he ever had any kids.

The Grouchy Ladybug and Other Stories

May 8, 2017

I suspect that most of you know exactly what I mean when I say that it makes you feel better to make someone else feel good. That's what happened to me one morning in mid-March after I drove to Rosedale Elementary School to read books to two grade school classes.

As I drift farther away from my elementary years—no, I didn't cipher on a slate or recite in a one-room "blab school"—I come to realize how much I miss the scent of crayons, the unfettered freedom of recess, and those great rainy afternoons spent with construction paper and LePage's white paste. I know that things have changed considerably over the years—

for instance, many children, unfortunately, now learn to read on tablets instead of feeling "real" books in their hands—but there is a warmness in an elementary school that you can get nowhere else; I sensed that all over again as soon as I walked through the doors that morning.

Since I was to choose my own books to read, I had Eric Carle's *The Grouchy Ladybug* and Gloria Houston's *My Great Aunt Arizona* tucked under my left arm, the first intended for Diana Martin's first-graders, and the second for Elizabeth Dickey's fourth-grade class. My wife, a perpetual smile now plastered on her face, for she is in the soon-to-be-retired phase of her career as an elementary librarian, recommended the first book. But the second is a personal favorite, not because I read it in grade school—it hadn't been written yet—but because I love its history and nostalgia.

I visited Mrs. Martin's classroom first, and walking through her door reminded me of what first grade is all about. Despite it also being "Pajama Day" —the students were decked out in flannel ninja pants, natty bath robes and pink house slippers—it was a squirming mass of restless legs and shouted questions. After a brief introduction (the most impressive part of my resume' being that I am "Mrs. Lunsford's husband"), the kids closed in and listened and participated in the reading.

If you haven't read it, *The Grouchy Ladybug* is about a rather bossy little beetle that spends much of its time challenging about every animal in the forest for superiority, all the time making itself a mouthy pest instead of a friend. A lesson in humility and sharing, the book was a hit with the students, many of whom chimed in with so many personal connections that I nearly ran out of reading time. After a quick photograph together, I had to shout a hasty goodbye as I hustled up the hallway to Grade 4.

It is with a touch of irony that I called Elizabeth Dickey, "Miss Dickey," when I came into her classroom. Not only is she a second cousin to my wife, but I recall her birth, see her every Sunday at church, and had her in my own classroom just a few years ago. She, like her students, was dressed in garb best suited for lounging, and because her kids are older and have more of an idea about rules and routine, they were a bit more resigned to listening to the old geezer who came to read to them.

Much to my surprise, the students seemed to like the book; a few asked questions about pot-bellied stoves and kerosene lamps, since both are included among the pictures. Many of the fourth-graders actually ran to get into positions when it came time for our picture. I know that had I been in their shoes, I would have just been happy there'd be less time left in the day for math lessons …

If you haven't noticed by now, I have yet to say how much better I hope my reading made the students feel that morning; I wasn't even sure it did until a few days later. That's when I received a number of letters voluntarily written by some of the kids who had listened to me, great youngsters like Zane and Matti, Caden and Joleen. Several even had accompanying artwork, right down to the blue sweater I wore for the occasion. I'm not sure what to think about Caden's picture, though. In it, I am either wearing a ball cap or have a graying "man bun" going.

Honestly, I wasn't having the best of days by the time I got to check my mailbox and saw the envelope from Rosedale amongst the usual junk. A dull headache, the hassles of grading term papers, and an epidemic of lethargy that often infects high school students in the spring, all had me considering a late career change—hermit, being one option. But, finding the letters in my slot helped me forget about that.

Joleen wrote: "I loved your book so much. … I love the books Mrs. Lunsford reads to us too. I have never read *My Aunt Arizona*, but I really liked it when you read it to us. … I think reading is important because you will do it all through your life."

Now, that made me feel better.

The Librarian Who Can Finally Sit Down

June 5, 2017

Joanie, retired last month and, typical of her, she is at school today "working on a few things" despite being officially finished with the job days ago.

After spending a decade or so in an English classroom, she changed jobs and took on that of being the librarian at our two elementary schools. Altogether, she put in 40 years, double the work load when you figure that she's also had to put up with Fred Flintstone for a husband.

Every other day, she bumped her way to one or the other of the schools, usually early, and stayed late and worked hard. She bought bargain books at garage sales, wrote grants to buy truckloads more, taped decrepit spines and repaired torn pages, and shelved and cataloged and ordered and reminded and reprimanded and taught and graded.

In other words, she showed the dedication most teachers do, and now, I am proud to know that she has run the race and fought the good fight, and has earned the right to sit down and read a few books for herself.

I know that there are many people out there who think they know what a teacher or school librarian does, but I don't take them very seriously because they have never done either job themselves. It is a profession that appears easy in theory, but isn't in reality. I've loved libraries my whole life, and had I not lived with a school librarian and seen the hours she put into her work, I would have thought that she did little more than stamp renewal cards and check for updates to the Dewey Decimal System.

But I will tell you this: I wouldn't have traded jobs with her for anything, and that comes from a man who collects books like a hoarder does used Tupperware and free insurance brochures.

Joanie loves books, but more importantly, she's spent most of her years in education loving the children she read those books to, bestowed books on, and worked so many hours for.

There wasn't a day that I can recall that she didn't have a story to tell me after she got home from work—most often three or four hours after the busses picked up the kids. Many of those tales were about rough days facing temper tantrums and upchucks, skinned knees and lost books, the time spent in after-school meetings that could have been better served dealing with stacks of returned books.

But most often her stories were about the blessings she had: the hugs and pleasant surprises, the unexpected gifts and random acts of kindness from co-workers, and, of course, from the children who treasured the book she'd given to them, some who said that the library was their favorite place to be.

I have had more than a few messy and frustrating days in my teaching life, but I honestly don't believe that I have had many that were as tough as hers were every day as she corralled kids at check-out time or shelved the hundreds of returned books alone or had after-school games clubs or filled out thousands of book orders or planned and organized hundreds of lesson plans. Her job, in my opinion, was something like calmly filling the Titanic's lifeboats…

I write this mostly in admiration for Joanie, but partially because I applaud anyone who sticks with teaching as long as she has, particularly for those who kept their faith in a less-than-perfect system, that worked doubly hard for kids they knew had little at home in the way of creature comforts or caring parents, and for those who believe that education isn't measured by profit margin or test scores. My wife was one of those kinds of teachers.

So, what comes next for someone who has spent most of her days teaching kids to be polite and kind? Someone who has raised a family, kept a poorly tempered husband in check, is conditioned to getting up at 5:30 a.m.? Well, I imagine she'll be plenty busy as a grandmother and wife, as volunteer and babysitter, and I know she plans to work on things that she has never had the time to work on before. She's already over getting out of bed that early.

But, I am certain that there will always be a part of her that will be a librarian. She will keep our "Little Library" in town filled with great titles, and she'll hand out books to kids like candy, and she'll read to our grandchildren, and will continue to believe—as the best teachers do—that a child who reads will never be bored.

And, she is finally going to have the time to sit down.

Field Notes and Other Stories

Mike Lunsford

Also by
MIKE LUNSFORD

The Off Season:
The Newspaper Stories of Mike Lunsford
ISBN 978-0-615-23811-1

Sidelines:
The Best of the Basketball Stories
ISBN 978-0-615-30731-2

A Place Near Home
ISBN 978-0-615-49749-5

A Windy Hill Almanac
ISBN 978-0-615-76553-2

The Bridge That Carries You Over
ISBN 978-0-692-46301-7